ESCRIMA MASTERS

By
Jose M. Fraguas

Disclaimer
Please note that the author and publisher of this book are NOT RESPONSIBLE in any manner whatsoever for any injury that may result from practicing the techniques and/or following the instructions given within. Since the physical activities described herein may be too strenuous in nature for some readers to engage in safely, it is essential that a physician be consulted prior to training.

First published in 2018 by Empire Books/AWP.

Copyright (c) 2018 by Empire Books/AWP LLC
All rights reserved. No part of this publication may be reproduced or utilized in any form or by any means, electronic or mechanical, including photocopying, recording, or by any information storage and retrieval system, without prior written permission from Empire Books/AWP LLC.

Library of Congress Cataloging-in-Publication Data

Names: Fraguas, Jose M., author.
Title: Escrima masters / by Jose M. Fraguas.
Description: Los Angeles, California : Empire Books, 2018.
Identifiers: LCCN 2018042812 | ISBN 9871949753059
Subjects: LCSH: Escrima. | Martial artists–Philippines–Interviews.
Classification: LCC GV1114.38 .F73 2018 | DDC 796.809599–dc23
LC record available at https://lccn.loc.gov/2018042812

Empire Books/AWP LLC
P.O. Box 401788
Los Angeles, CA 90049

First edition
18 17 16 15 14 13 12 11 10

Printed in the United States of America

"Before a fight, I go to mountains alone. I pretend my enemy is there. I imagine being attacked, and in my imagination I fight for real. I keep this up until my mind is ready for the kill. I can't lose. When I enter the ring, nobody can beat me; I already know that man is beaten."

Floro Villabrille

Dedication

I dedicate this book to Guro Daniel Inosanto.

Acknowledgments

Many people were responsible for making this book possible, some more directly than others. I want to extend my gratitude to all those whom so generously contributed their time and experience to the preparation of this work. A very special thanks to my teacher, Dan Inosanto, whose flights of guidance throughout my Escrima/Kali/Arnis life and Martial Arts journey, have been always on the wings of excitement and self-discovery. Special thanks to Joshua Ryder for the images contribution in the chapter of Master Cacoy Canete.

To all the instructors who shared their knowledge and experience with me, past and present, for giving me the understanding and knowledge to undertake all the Filipino Martial Arts projects I've done during my life. My understanding of the art has grown over the years thanks to the questions they made me ask myself. These questions — both perceptive and practical — have sent me further and deeper in search for answers. This book would not exist without you.

You all have my enduring thanks.

— Jose M. Fraguas

About the Author

Born and raised in Madrid, Spain, Jose M. Fraguas began his martial arts studies with judo, in grade school, at age 9. From there he moved to study to other arts. In 1980, he moved to Los Angeles, California, where his open-minded mentality helped him to develop a more elaborated approach to the martial arts. His training in Filipino Martial Arts started that year at the old "Kali Academy" owned by Guro Dan Inosanto in Torrance, California. His Escrima journey and tutelage under Guro Inosanto led him to train with other legendary masters from whom he learned different Kali and Arnis approaches and methods to the Filipino Martial Arts. He began his career as a writer at age 16 as a regular contributor to martial arts magazines in Great Britain, France, Spain, Italy, Germany, Portugal, Holland and Australia. In 1980, he moved to Los Angeles, California, where his open-minded mentality helped him to develop a more elaborated approach to the martial arts.

Fraguas founded his first publishing company in Europe, authoring dozens of books and distributing his magazines to 35 countries in five different languages. His reputation and credibility as a martial artist and publisher became well known to the top masters around the world. Considering himself a martial artist first and a writer and publisher second, Fraguas feels fortunate to have had the opportunity to interview many legendary martial artists. He recognizes that much of the information given in the interviews helped him to discover new dimensions in the martial arts. "I was constantly absorbing knowledge from the great masters," he recalls. "I only trained with a few of them, but intellectually, academically and spiritually all of them have made very important contributions to my growth as a complete martial artist."

Steeped in tradition yet looking to the future, Fraguas understands and appreciates martial arts history and philosophy and feels this rich heritage is a necessary steppingstone to personal growth and spiritual evolution. His desire to promote both ancient philosophy and modern thinking provided the motivation for writing this book. "If the motivation is just money, a book cannot be of good quality," Fraguas says. "If the book is written to just make people happy, it cannot be deep. I want to write books so I can learn as well as teach. Martial Arts, like human life itself, are filled with experiences that seem quite ordinary at the time and assume a fabled stature only with the passage of the years. I hope this work will be appreciated by future practitioners not only of the Filipino Martial Arts but for all martial arts in general, regardless of the style."

It is clear that every one of us will some kind of leave a legacy behind when we die. The challenge is the same for all of us. For Fraguas, who has authored more than 30 books, the important question is what kind of legacy will I leave? "I believe our main legacy as writers is to educate or even just re-echo those things that we believe are worthwhile - a subjective matter. Even if the idea is obvious or simple, we believe it deserves to be kept alive, and we do that using different ways current with the times; we broadcast our worldview with our family, friends, co-workers, and so on," he says. "Ideally we live by our beliefs so as to lend them credence; the "unfollowing adherent" is just a meaningless mouthpiece - a preacher not following his own sermon. A legacy of values proven out by the bearer's own life would be a very good legacy for anyone. Life is motion, and the real goal of a writer should be to arrest that motion [which is life] and preserve knowledge [the words of these masters in this book] by artificial means, and hold it fixed so that a hundred years later, when a stranger opens a book and reads it, it moves again since it is life. Since man is mortal, the only immortality possible for a writer is to leave something behind him that is immortal since it will always move. This is the writer's way of scribbling "I was here" on the wall of the final and irrevocable oblivion through which we all must someday pass."

Jose M. Fraguas lives in Los Angeles, California.

Introduction

Some of my best days were spent interviewing and meeting with the Escrima & Kali masters in this book. There is little I enjoy more than reading a great interview while time slows and sometimes even seems to stop. Having the opportunity to meet and interview the most prestigious Filipino martial Arts icons of the past five decades is something that every martial artist doesn't have the chance to do. Hopefully, in some small way, this will help make up for that. Meeting the masters and having long conversations with them allowed me to do more than simply scratch the surface of the technical aspects of the art; it also allowed me to understand the human beings behind the teachers. Some of the dialogues and interviews began by simply commenting about the superficial techniques of fighting, and ended up turning into a spiritual conversation about the philosophical aspects of the Filipino Martial Arts. Although these masters are all very different, they share a common thread of traditional values such as discipline, respect, positive attitude, dedication and etiquette.

For more than 40 years I've interviewed great masters, one-on-one, face-to-face, with no place to run if I asked a stupid question. Many times it was a real challenge to not just talk to them, but to make the questions interesting enough to bring out their deepest knowledge. I tried to absorb as much knowledge as I could, ranging from their training methods, to their system, to their philosophies about life itself. Their personal cultural backgrounds never prevented them from analyzing, researching or modifying anything they considered important. They always kept their minds open to improving the art and themselves. From a formal philosophical point of view, many of them followed classical philosophies and religions—but they all tempered that with vast amounts of common sense.

They devoted themselves to the Filipino Arts, often in solitude, to the exclusion of other "normal" pursuits. They worked themselves into extraordinary physical condition. They ignored distractions and diversions and concentrated on their mental and physical training. They got as good as they could possibly get at performing and teaching the art while the rest of us watched them, leading our "balanced lives," and wondering how good we might have gotten at something had we devoted ourselves to it as ferociously as these masters embraced their journey. In that respect, they bear our dreams.

If you read carefully between the lines, you'll see that none of these men were trying to become a fighting machine, or create the most devastating martial arts system known to man. They focused, rather, on how to use the arts to become a better person. There are many principles that once discovered open a wide spectrum of possibilities, not only to the fighting arts, but to a better existence as individuals.

The interviews often lasted as long as three or four hours. I would begin at their school and finish the conversation at a restaurant or coffee shop. Much of this information had never been published before and some had to be trimmed either at the master's request or edited to avoid misunderstandings. It is not the questions that make an interview. An interview is either good or bad depending on the answers. Considering the masters in this book, I had an easy job. My goal was to make them comfortable talking about life and Escrima training.

"The great old masters are gone," many like to say. But as long as we keep their teachings in our heart, they will live forever. To understand the Filipino Martial Arts properly, it is necessary to take into account its philosophical methods as well as its physical techniques. There is a deep distinction between a fighting system and a martial art. Unfortunately, the roots of arts have been de-emphasized, neglected or totally abandoned today. Escrima is not a sport, although it can be useful as such in our modern society. Someone who chooses to devote himself to a sport such as basketball, tennis, soccer or football—which is based on youth, strength, and speed—chooses to die twice. When you can no longer do

that sport, due to the lack of their required attributes, waking up in the morning without the activity that has been the center of your life for 35 years is troubling and unsettling. In contrast, the Filipino Martial Arts can and should be practiced for life—it never leaves you.

All the masters have expressed similar ideas in very different ways. Regardless of the words they used, there must be truth in the philosophies and principles that so many different people have believed in and lived by — and in some cases — died for. The more I interviewed them, the more I realized that those great masters are more like you and me than they are different. They had difficult days and seemingly impossible hurdles, yet they endured and prevailed. Most of what passed as human wisdom is merely the post-examination gabble of excited individuals trying to guess how the new lessons will explain the old questions of life and martial arts training. Anything is fresh on the first hearing ... even though others may have heard it a thousand times through a score of generations.

A true practitioner is like a musician, painter, writer or actor—their art is an expression of themselves. The need to discover who they are becomes the reason for an endless search for the perfect technique, great melody, inspiring poetry, amazing painting or Academy Award performance. It is this motivation to reach that impossible dream that allows a simple individual to become an exceptional artist and master of his craft. Many of the greatest teachers share a commonly misunderstood teaching methodology. They know the words they could use to teach their students have little or no meaning. They know that to try "self-discovery" in quantitative or empirical terms is a useless task. A great deal of knowledge and wisdom comes from oral traditions, which Filipino Martial Arts, like every other cultural expression, has. These oral traditions have always been reserved for a certain kind of student and considered "secrets," given only to a special few who have the minds and attitudes to fully grasp them. Alexandra David-Neel wrote: "It is not on the master that the secret depends but on the hearer. Truth learned from others is of no value, the only truth which is effective and of value is self-discovered … the teacher can only guide to the point of discovery." In the end, "the only secret is that there is no secret." As Kato Tokuro, arguably the finest potter of the last century, a great art scholar, and the teacher of Pablo Picasso said: "The sole cause of secrets in craftsmanship is the student's inability to learn." To find out what the Filipino Martial Arts mean to you, what it does for you, and what it holds for you, is a deeply personal process. Each path is different and we all have to find a personal rhythm that fit us individually, according to what surround us.

As human beings, we are always tempted to follow linear logic towards ultimate self-improvement—but the truth is that there are no absolute truths. You have to find your own way in life whether it be in martial arts, business or cherry picking. Whatever path you pursue, you have to distill the personal truths that are right for you, according to your own nature. The quest for perfection is very imperfect, and not in tune with human nature or experience. To have any hope of attaining even a single perfection, you have to concentrate on a single pursuit and direct all your energy towards it. In this sense, perfection comes from appreciating endeavors for their own sake—not to impress anyone—but for your own inner satisfaction and sense of accomplishment. It is important to have a feeling of responsibility; and putting yourself into an art as genuinely as you can, without any sense that you are going to get something back in return, reverberates throughout time and space. We need to honor those who came before us, as well as nurture those who will come after, so the art can grow and expand—you've got to send the elevator back down.

Martial Arts are a large part of my life and I draw inspiration from it. I really don't know the "how" or the "why" of its effect on me, but I feel its influence in even my most mundane activities. All human beings have sources or principles that keep them grounded, and the Martial Arts is mine. That is when the term "way of life" becomes real. In bushido, the self-discipline required to pursue mastery is more

important than mastery itself—the struggle is more important than the reward. A common thread throughout the lives of all the masters appearing in this book is their constant struggle towards self-mastery. They realized that life is an ongoing process, and once you achieve all your goals you are as good as dead. But this process is not all driven by action. Often the greatest action is inaction, and the hardest voice to hear is the sound of your own thoughts. You need to sit alone and collect yourself, free from technology and distraction, and just think. This is perhaps the only way to achieve mental and spiritual clarity.

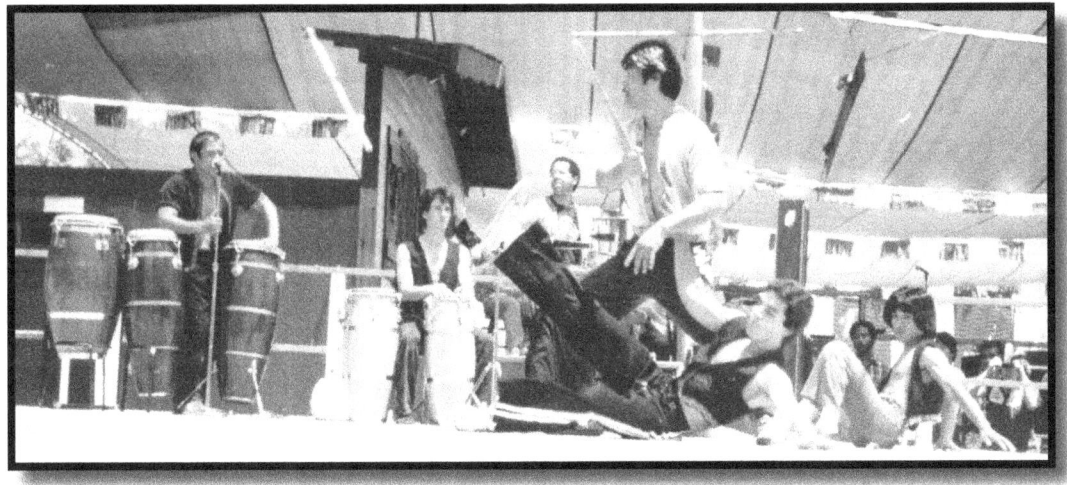

I don't believe that books are meant to be read fast. I've always thought that writing is timeless and that reading is not a detraction. So take your time. Books are an essential part of our existence and they open new and exciting avenues of life. My goal is to share these interviews with as many people as possible. I hope this collection provides comfort and inspiration for the Escrima practitioner, the martial artist — regardless of style — and for the casual reader. If you, the reader, find this work useful as both a guide and a reference work and discover some unexpected thoughts and philosophies, the book will have served its purpose. Approach this book with the Zen "beginner's mind" and "empty cup" mentality and soak up the words of these great Filipino Martial Arts teachers. They will help you to not only grow as a martial artist but as a human being as well.

Contents

1 CRISPULO ATILLO
THE POWER OF BALINTAWAK ESCRIMA

7 ALFREDO BANDALAN
THE SPIRIT OF DOCE PARES

13 RICHARD BUSTILLO
THE REAL "IRON MAN"

21 CACOY CANETE
THE ESKRIMA LEGEND

27 VIRGIL CAVADA
INTO THE BLADE

35 LEO M. GIRON
THE LAST OF THE BLADED WARRIORS

45 DAN INOSANTO
THE ETERNAL MASTER AND THE FOREVER STUDENT

51 BEN LARGUSA
A SIMPLE MAN OF KALI

63 RENE LATOSA
A HIGHER LEVEL OF MARTIAL ART

73 SEAN LONTAYAO
A FAMILY JOURNEY

83 CHRIS RICKETTS
KALI ILUSTRISIMO – THE ORIGINAL WAY

89 TONY SOMERA
A HIGHER CALLING

95 EDGAR G. SULITE
THE LEGACY OF STEEL

99 DARREN G. TIBON
ANGEL'S DISCIPLES

107 MARK V. WILEY
ON FILIPINO MARTIAL ARTS

119 EPILOGUE
ESCRIMA – THE HIDDEN TREASURE BY ANTONIO E. SOMERA

CRISPULO ATILLO

THE POWER OF BALINTAWAK ESCRIMA

GRANDMASTER CRISPULO "ISING" ATILLO IS THE LIVING ENBODIMENT OF THE TRADITIONAL ESCRIMA MASTER: EXCELLENT TECHNICIAN, QUIET, AND ABOVE ALL, A GENTLEMAN. A TRUE ENCYCLOPEDIA OF THE FILIPINO OF ATILLO BALINTAWAK, BASED ON THE METHOD OF THE LEGENDARY ESCRIMADOR DORING SAAVEDRA, GRANDMASTER ATILLO HAS DEDICATED ALL HIS LIFE TO THE PRACTICE AND STUDY OF THE ARTS OF ESCRIMA AND ARNIS. STRIVING FOR A LIFE OF CONTENTMENT AND TRANQUILITY, GRANDMASTER ATILLO PURSUES HIS ESCRIMA JOURNEY WITH TOTAL DISCIPLINE, COMMITMENT AND PASSION. DESPITE HIS BUSY SCHEDULE, GRANDMASTER ATILLO STILL TEACHES THE ART OF ESCRIMA ON A REGULAR BASIS NOT ONLY TO NEW STUDENTS BUT TO OTHER ESCRIMA, KALI, AND ARNIS MASTERS AS WELL.

How long have you been practicing karate?

I have been practicing the art of Eskrima since I was 14 years old; that was way back in 1952. I am 71 years old right now. I was the youngest member of the group called Balintawak established in 1952. My father, Vicente "Inting" Atillo, also was one of the original members.

Today, the Atillo System is Balintawak, but I added to it what I found over the years to be more useful and removed what I thought was useless. Atillo Balintawak is a powerful Filipino martial art developed by me based on the style of legendary Grandmaster Doring Saavedra. This art focuses on stick fighting and its application with bladed weapons, as well as empty hands. Efficiency and power are put together to produce this fighting system. It is a highly efficient style in actual and tournament situations.

What were the teaching methods like?

When I began learning the art of Eskrima, the methods of teaching were totally different than the methods of teaching today. For one, in 1952, when I started, it was mostly a one-on-one type of teaching, teacher and student. There was no specific method of teaching to follow, like a set of fundamentals, so it was harder to understand. Also, most teachers during the period would hit the students just to let them feel the pain.

ESCRIMA MASTERS

Today, you cannot just hit the student just to make a point in your teaching. You still can hit but it is a much more controlled type of hit. Also, students are given a set of exercises to follow and it is much easier to learn the art of Eskrima. Still, it is not as easy to learn the Art of Eskrima as it looks. In general, it is a lot easier for students to learn any martial arts today, as compared to many years ago. What is required is just the thirst for knowledge in that particular field of martial arts.

Do you have a particularly memorable experience?

My most memorable experience was my first actual fight. I was sent a letter of challenge by my opponent, and I accepted it. It was a death match, meaning no headgear or any body protectors were allowed, and it happened in 1964, when I was 26 years old. My father, Vicente "Inting" Atillo, was present during the fight.

How has your perception of the art and training in Eskrima developed over the years?

When you are always teaching and practicing the art of Eskrima, you also will improve yourself, in terms of developing new techniques and teaching style and also personal growth like increase awareness, patience, and understanding. I developed a more advanced system of teaching over the years and credit my constant teaching and practice for that improvement. When you also practice regularly, you will discover more techniques on how to attack and disarm your opponents.

What are the specifics aspects that make your Escrima style unique?

In general, the Balintawak style of Eskrima already is unique. In particular, I could mention at least three areas where my style of Eskrima is unique:

1. Foot movement – our feet are constantly changing directions, depending upon where the strikes are coming from or the position of the opponent's feet.
2. Hands – Both the left and right hands are moving constantly during the sparring or fight; they never rest.
3. Defense – Our style is very defense-oriented. Our stick is always vertical and the left or right, depending on if you are left or right-handed, is always behind the stick hand.

Our motto is to hit, but not to be hit.

Do you think there still is a "pure" system of Kali and Eskrima, or we are going to a more "mixed" approach?

In our style, we are using a pure Filipino system of Eskrima. My students call me a purist, because I do not combine other styles of martial arts in my teaching. You easily can add and mix other styles of martial arts to Eskrima, like Judo or Boxing, but I prefer to teach the real pure art of Eskrima. It also depends on what the students want to learn, as some like to learn the pure art of Eskrima and others want to mix it up with so many other styles of martial arts. Of course, I gave in every now and then and show my students how to incorporate other martial arts styles into our Eskrima, especially on countering other styles.

What are the major changes in the arts since you began training?

One major change is the way students are taught. When I started training, there was no specific path to follow on what to learn next. It was a come-as-you-go method: whatever the teacher can think of or wants, you follow. Today, students have it a lot easier. They are taught certain movements and after they master it, they move on to the next level. The modern age also has affected how Eskrima is being taught. When I started, access to a camera or video equipment was limited or very expensive; therefore learning was a lot harder. Nowadays, with all the modern technology, a student easily can learn the art of Eskrima. Still one major characteristic, has not changed since the beginning and that is the thirst for knowledge in learning the art of Eskrima. Without it, any modern technology assistance is useless.

How do you think a practitioner can increase his or her understanding of the spiritual aspects of the arts?

Any student in whatever martial art they are studying easily can increase his or her understanding of the spiritual aspects of the art by connecting what they have learned and apply it to their daily lives, especially in their relationship with other people and the one they love. Some students practice martial arts to control their emotions and to keep calm in extreme situations. They easily can apply all the traits to become good martial artists, in their day-to-day life. By doing so, he or she will become a much better person in general.

Do you think that the technical level of the Filipino Arts in the West has caught up to the level of the Philippines?

The Philippines is still far more advanced as to the technical level than the West, and I am talking about our style, which is Atillo Balintawak – Saavedra style. It will be awhile before the West can catch up with the Philippines, especially on Balintawak style. However, the West, because of its intense desire to study the art, spends a lot of time practicing the art of Eskrima as compared to the Philippines. In other sports, like Judo and Tae Kwon Do, a majority of young people in Japan and Korea practices the art, but in the Philippines, it is a different story. Being colonized for more than 400 years has left Filipinos with a feeling of inferiority that still is prevalent today, especially in sports.

It hurts me personally that people from foreign countries are so eager and hungry to learn the art of Eskrima because they see its effectiveness, while Filipinos fail to see what is available locally and in front of their eyes.

Are martial arts a sport or a way of life?

I will say that it depends on a particular student. I have students who practice martial arts just to become proficient in that sport in terms of movements, but do not correlate it to their daily habits and attitudes. On the other hand, for a lot of my students, it is a way of life. They really practice what the art is all about. Respect, self-control, and perseverance are just some of the traits that they bring from learning the art into their daily lives. They incorporate what they learn in terms of discipline into their lives and their relationships with loved ones and friends.

I always emphasize to my students the proper behavior when practicing the art, for students who lack the proper traits will not advance and will drop out in less than one year. I can guide them to become a much better Eskrimador and fighter, but they must be willing to spend enough time to practice on their own while at the same time having a balanced, well-rounded family life.

Do you think it helps students to train with weapons?

Eskrima is one of the few martial arts in the world, if not the only one, in which a beginner student is given a weapon – in this case a stick – when he or she starts learning, so I can say with authority that it helps a lot. Eskrima is a weapon-based system and it has a big advantage for students in terms of improving their hand and eye coordination. When the Spanish conquistadores invaded the Philippines in 1521, the Filipino warriors were fighting them with bladed weapons, using single- or double-edge swords. Spanish firearms and their use of local rivals (divide and conquer) were able to overwhelm the Filipinos. They then imposed a ban on the use of bladed weaponry and anyone caught using them or practicing Filipino martial arts was thrown in jail and accused of being a rebel. The Filipinos improvised by incorporating Filipino martial art movements in dances and religious rituals.

Who would you like to have trained with that you have not, and why?

I have no specific person in my mind that I would have liked to teach. In general, I am willing to teach anyone who aspires to learn this unique style of Eskrima. Every time a prospective student calls me or visits me, I am so happy, because my main goal is to teach and spread the art of Eskrima around the world, not just any Eskrima but Atillo Balintawak – Saavedra style. Anybody can learn this art; all that is needed is the desire to learn . For that, the student must make the first step.

What keeps you motivated to train after all these years?

I want to be remembered around the world as that person who taught the art of Eskrima – Atillo Balintawak, Saavedra style. I want them to learn my style so that every time they practice they will remember me when I pass away someday. Some of my students, after a few years or even months of learning the art of Eskrima, think they already are experts or have enough knowledge of the art.

I will tell you, even I am still learning after 60 years of studying and teaching the art.

Techniques can be improved, disarms can be countered a different way, and overall knowledge can be improved. So, learning the art of Eskrima is a lifetime commitment, even for me.

Do you think no-holds-barred (MMA) events bring positive or negative aspects to the martial arts?

Mixed Martial Arts is a good way to promote various styles of martial arts in one big venue. People, especially the ones who practice different styles of martial arts, are divided on the issue. Some do not like MMA because they think it degrades their particular martial arts style; others like MMA because they can see how their styles are put to the test and mixed with other styles. It is up to the student to choose which style of martial arts they want to practice and follow. In the end, it is the general public that determines if MMA will prosper or not.

What are your thoughts on the future of Filipino Martial arts and of your style in the USA?

If students will continue to learn and practice Filipino martial arts in general and Atillo Balintawak—Saavedra style in particular, then it will just grow bigger and bigger every year and will expand outside the U.S. We get a lot of inquiries about where to find the nearest Atillo Balintawak – Saavedra style training centers. For me, Filipino martial arts still is in its infancy around the world. Filipino martial arts has made a big step forward the past ten years, but it still has a lot of ground to cover, in terms of acceptance and popularity.

Do you have any general advice to pass on?

Live life to the fullest and learn how to control your emotions even in extreme situations.

Do not brag about your knowledge of any martial art or start a fight just to show them.

Practicing any form of martial art is a lifetime commitment, if you want to be good at it. You cannot say to yourself that in five years I will become a Master and then stop. It does not work that way . Keep learning. Keep practicing.

ALFREDO BANDALAN

THE SPIRIT OF DOCE PARES

Grandmaster Alfredo Bandalan Sr. was born in Hawaii on the Island of Lanai in 1939. His introduction to Eskrima came at the hands of his grandfather, Pedro Blanko, who was from Mandawi, Cebu, the Philippines. Although his grandfather never actually taught him Eskrima, feeling it too dangerous an art, Grandmaster Bandalan did catch glimpses of his grandfather's Eskrima style during demonstrations at family gatherings and when he played childish pranks on his grandfather.

In 1958, he graduated from Honolulu City College. He started working for the Honolulu Welding Co. when he met his first martial arts teacher, Master Philip Doseo of Kajukenbo. In 1968 Grandmaster Bandalan immigrated to San Jose, California, where he continued has martial arts training under the guidance of Chief Instructor Sam Brown of the Black Ram school.

In 1975, he met Grandmaster Angel Cabales in Livingston, California, and trained with him and his Guro, Mike Inay. He continued his training in Hawaian Kenpo, and in 1975, Professor Marino Tiwanak awarded him his black belt. In 1976, Professor Tiwanak, founder of the Central Hawaiian Activities III (C.H.A. III.), awarded Grandmaster Bandalan his Chief Instructor ranking and designated him head of the San Jose Chapter of C.H.A. III Kenpo.

Grandmaster Bandalan, along with Ed Abinsay and Leo Fernandez, promoted the First National Eskrima Tournament in San Jose, California. From this tournament, the Regional, National, and the World Tournaments was born, which today is WEKAF. He also became Assistant Coach to the First World Tournament and ever since has been participating actively in subsequent WEKAF World Championships, along with other WEKAF-related activities. Grandmaster Bandalan is considered the Doce Pares founding member in the United States.

ESCRIMA MASTERS

How long have you been practicing martial arts?

For more than 56 years. I graduated in 1956 from Lanai High School I in Hawaii. My first passion was boxing and during my last years in high school, I took boxing under the CYO – Catholic Youth Organization. After graduating high school, my father told me boxing or education. I ended up going to Honolulu Technical and when I graduated I began working for Hawaii Welding Company in 1959. One day I was told by my supervisor to go to Gaspro Company and pick up some supplies and while I was there I met a gentleman named Philip Doreo. He took out his wallet and asked if I was interested in taking karate. I was shocked and said yes because in those days you didn't join, you were invited. We must remember Kenpo in Hawaii still was in its infancy stage. He became my first teacher in Kenpo. In 1968, I moved to San Jose, California, and joined Professor Sam Brown of the Kenpo BonAi. I hold a Deputy Professor and I also hold a Chief Instructor rank from Professor Marino of C.H.A. III.

My Escrima training began in early 1975. I was the first Filipino American to be invited by the famed Doce Pares of Cebu. There, I met Grandmaster Diony Canete and Cacoy Canete and the senior Canete. On January 4, 1987, I was given affiliation papers by the Doce Pares club, signed by Cacoy Canete, Euldgio Canete, Filemon Canete, and Diony Canete.

How did you get involved with the Doce Pares method of Escrima?

I felt that Eskrima in America was limited. Early in 1977, I wrote to the Philippines asking for information on Eskrima and my letter was forwarded to Doce Pares. I received a reply from Grandmaster Cacoy Canete and within a month Grandmaster Diony Canete arrived in San Jose and I received my first training in Doce Pares. Later on, I flew to Cebu and was greeted by all the Doce Pares masters. For twenty years, I trained with Cacoy and Diony Canete. In 1981 Diony Canete told me to name my school – Bandalan Doce Pares. I also became President of the United States Arnis, Kali, Eskrima Federation, affiliated with National Arnis of the Philippines (NARAPHIL), and later a founding member of World Eskrima Kali Arnis Federation (WEKAF).

What were the teaching methods like?

In Kenpo during the early 1950s, we always would begin with a prayer and end with a prayer. The philosophy and history was mostly verbal. The training was brutal, with busted teeth, cheekbones sliced open, and, if you didn't end the night with bruises, then you were not trained hard enough. That was the mentality of the fifties and one must remember Kenpo in Hawaii was still in its infancy stage. In Escrima in the early 1970s, the Doce Pares club was highly in-depth in its teaching; it had different levels of Senior Instructors to teach before a Grandmaster would come in. The only difference at that time was that the live stick sparring still had the mentality of a death match and it was full contact.

One memory that stands out was my first night training in the Philippines in the famed Doce Pares club. This older Filipino instructor called me over to cross stick – and wham, I felt a hit on my lower body and I fell flat on my face. I looked up and I could see his eyes roll back; I thought he was going to kill me. I heard Cacoy yell at him, "Slow down, Fred is here to train." I later found out his name was Anting Carin.

How has your perception of the art and training in Escrima developed over the years?

Very in-depth because I have had a better understanding of the art, its culture, philosophy. and history – and listening and watching the old masters go through their spiritual and physical workouts and the aura that they project.

Do you think there still is a pure system of Kali and Escrima, or are we going to a more mixed approach?

This is a debatable question. I find that through my travels to the Philippines, I have met many Masters who don't want to change; yet, other Masters have changed. I believe there still are some pure systems of Escrima; for instance, Grandmaster Diony still practices the old San Miguel style, Grandmaster Cacoy has the modified system, which never has changed to this day, and Grandmaster's Remy Presas Jr. and Grandmaster Vince Caballas still teach the old system. Even in Hawaii, there still are the old Kali. To me, this is all pure, but we must remember there are some Masters who do take the mixed approach.

What are the major changes in the art since you began training?

Everything has changed in the way Martial Arts are being taught regarding Escrima. It peaked in the 1990s and today is slow in progression, but many Karate and other Martial Arts schools now are implementing Escrima in their curriculum; even the movie industry has taken an interest in Filipino arts.

ESCRIMA MASTERS

How do you think the practitioners can increase their understanding of the spiritual aspect of the art?

First and foremost, there is a new generation of practitioners and teachers. We have lost the aspect of spiritual training here in America; however, in my view, there are schools in the Orient that still teach "spiritual" and deep meditation, and it's quite possible there are still schools in America that have it in their system. Of course, it all depends on each individual to do his or her homework and deep research in finding a style that offers deep meditation, and meets one's needs spiritually and physically in their daily lives.

Do you think that Filipino Martial Arts in the West has caught up to the level of the Philippines?

This is another debatable question. My feeling is, I don't think so. In some areas, the West may have caught up due to its high technology, but at this very moment the European countries in large numbers are visiting the Philippines for training. I have witnessed much training in the headquarters of Doce Pares. Consider the fact that when WEKAF holds its World tournament in the Philippines, more than 30 countries will attend, so the West has work to do to catch up.

Are Martial Arts a sport or a way of life?

There are two kinds of Martial Arts – traditional and non-traditional. The non-traditional is geared for tournaments only; the traditional Martial Arts promotes character building, leadership, and disci-

BANDALAN

pline. As Gichin Funukoshi once said: "A true black belt is someone who has mastered everything under the sun; last but not least is a Humanitarian."

Do you think it helps students to train with weapons?

Very much so. You see, many schools are implementing weapons in their curriculum, especially Escrima. It helps their confidence and gives them the feeling of added power. It's also common knowledge that someone who knows how to use an Escrima stick can control 5–10 attackers within seconds traveling at 120 miles.

Who would you like to train with that you have not and why?

The man who walked this earth 2,000 years ago – Jesus Christ. To learn the way of life, peace, and happiness, the respect of your fellow man and to love your enemy and walk away from confrontations.

What keeps you motivated to train all these years?

Seeing the success of all of my students and watching them become successful parents. Listening and helping people of all walks of life; watching the old Masters training daily spiritually and physically and the aura they project: all of this gives me much incentive in my training.

Do you think MMA events bring positive or negative aspects to the Martial Arts?

First of all, I have nothing against an MMA event. This is America; someone always will come up with an idea of excitement and to make money. But, something has to be done because you have kids who will copy some of these no-holds-barred brutal techniques and use them to bully other schoolkids, creating a juvenile delinquent. Martial Arts teaches everyone the respect of each other, how to walk away from a fight, and how to achieve love and unity.

Do you have general advice to pass on?

Enjoy life every minute of the day. Deeply immerse yourself in reading Escrima history, philosophy, and spirituality – then apply it to your daily life.

RICHARD BUSTILLO

THE REAL "IRON MAN"

Hawaiian-born Richard Bustillo wass one of the few men chosen to privately train in Jeet Kune Do with Bruce Lee. A former kajukenbo practitioner, Bustillo was earned the nickname of "The Iron Man of JKD." He was the man in charge of showing the door to all those who were abusing the knowledge taught at the old "Filipino Kali Academy" in Torrance, California. Known for his warm sense of humor, Richard "Iron Man" Bustillo was the man one didn't cross.

Grandmaster Bustillo spent over 45 years studying martial arts from his base in Los Angeles, the IMB (International Martial Arts and Boxing). His credits are almost too numerous to mention. He trained with some of the greatest martial artists of our generation. Whether studying Jeet Kune Do with Bruce Lee or Kajukenbo with Sid Asuncion; Judo with Henry Okazaki or Escrima with Cacoy Canete, Bustillo was a willing and grateful student.

Bustillo was one of the leading forces in the Filipino Martial Arts expansion. Retired after 20 years of employment with Continental Airlines, Bustillo remained deeply committed to martial arts and the art and philosophy of Filipino Martial Arts and Bruce Lee's Jeet Kune Do

---

Master Bustillo, please tell us about your martial arts background?

I did train in several disciplines Doce Pares Eskrima, Wrestling, Muay Thai, (USA Boxing coach and official), Kali and Arnis, Jun Fan Jeet Kune Do and other Martial Arts. But these we can consider to be my base and foundation.

How were your early days in Hawaii and why you started training?

I grew up in Hawaii. In Hawaii we ran around bare footed, and I trained in judo for a year when I was a kid or so until my family relocated to another town. Where we settled was a boxing school where

ESCRIMA MASTERS

most of my new friends went, so I joined them. Although many kids give up martial arts in their teens, I kept on because of my environment. I grew up in the housing projects with a brother and 4 sisters. My Dad wanted me to learn how to protect myself so that's what I did. Of course I trained in the art of Kajubenbo and Kenpo. This early training and its teachings have stayed with me until today and helped me immensely to understand everything else that I studied afterwards.

You studied kenpo before going into Filipino Martial Arts, right?

Yes. But I felt it really limiting. Because of my boxing background I was always on the balls of my feet. When I was studying kajukenbo the instructors kept telling me to be flat-footed. I couldn't! They were preventing me from going my own way and tried to make me fit their way. Sometimes you have to break tradition and question a few things in order to find yourself.

But kajukenbo seems to be a very free and liberated.

Yes, it is. But the problem was that the kajukenbo system stays within the limits of the methods used in the style. You can't break away from those and express yourself totally. The main idea is there but it is not taken to that level.

When did you start your training in the Filipino Martial Arts?

My start in the Filipino martial arts started when I was training with Bruce Lee. Dan Inosanto and I were training under him at the Lee Jun Fan Gung Fu Institute in Chinatown Los Angeles, when Dan asked me if I knew anything about the Filipino art of Eskrima. I told him that I'd seen an Eskrima performance and I wasn't really interested. I just wanted to learn more of Bruce Lee's Jeet Kune Do. One day he invited me to do with him to Stockton, California to visit Grandmaster Angel Cabales. Dan's parents lived in Stockton and had set up a private lesson for us with GM Angel Cabales. In the beginning, I wasn't too excited about Eskrima; however, it was Dan who said to me that I should have patience, and keep training. All I can say is that our personal research and studies far exceeded our expectations in the Filipino martial arts. Today, Dan and I are given credit worldwide for reviving and promoting the Filipino martial arts.

What did you find so attractive about FMA?

I really think that Filipino martial arts are among the best self-defense methods when practicing with or without a weapon. Their methods of training with weapons build a strong foundation in one's mental and physical abilities. It gives the individual the psychological edge of understanding how empty hand can be used against weapons and how to efficiently use weapons for self-defense.

When did you meet Bruce Lee for the first time?

I met Bruce in 1964 during an exhibition host by Ed Parker in Long Beach at the "Ed Parker's Karate Internationals". Bruce emphasized that "the individual is always more important than a system or a style." And I truly believed that. I carefully listened to what he said and all made sense to me as a martial artist.

Having been trained traditionally where everybody does everything the same I knew that adaptability was the key to effectiveness. Bruce was really focusing on that and I decided to follow him. Bruce's philosophy and the principles and concepts of jeet kune do were something I always believed in from the first time I met him. Training with Bruce was a very revealing experience because he made you aware of you own capabilities. He'd help you to discover your strengths and weaknesses.

Dan Inosanto and you were the leaders in the development of the Filipino Arts in America and also the rest of the world. Would you tell us how all started?

Many of the Filipino Arts had not a set curriculum like other arts. They never were taught that way. It was difficult for other martial artists whom were trained in a more traditional way to understand this concept. We used the vehicle of teaching seminars to start introducing the arts and the training methods

ESCRIMA MASTERS

to other martial artists. We incorporated weaponry training and showed them how the weapons can drastically improve your empty hand skills. Personally I started to add a more cohesive structure to what I was teaching, Muay Thai and Boxing for my striking middle range, and my Wrestling and Jujitsu for my grappling close range training. This allowed me to integrate all ranges for my self-defense system. Bruce Lee always taught that an individual should be well rounded in all martial arts ranges, not just the kicking, not just the hands, not just the grappling and not just the weaponry.

What can you tell us about Dan Inosanto?

Dan Inosanto not only is my teacher but for me is alike a brother. I have been very fortunate to have a friend, training partner, teacher and brother for all this time. He is one of the kindest, most generous and honest people I have ever known in my life and as a martial artist is a true martial arts encyclopedia. He always wants to study and learn more about different arts. He is never satisfied. I have seen him make many sacrifices for the martial arts knowledge he has acquired. Bruce saw something special in him and that was the reason why Bruce wanted him to be the Instructor in his Los Angeles Chinatown "kwoon". Dan Inosanto once told me, "We are lucky to have met Bruce Lee." And I answered "Yes." And he said, "No, I mean because of that we met each other." Our lifestyle have changed throughout the years and us with it. Like it or not, that's what life is all about – change. You can't avoid it.

It is true that after Bruce died Dan wanted to stop and finally you decided to keep going?

Yes. Both of us were devastated by Bruce's death. Dan wanted to quit martial arts completely. I told him that if he quit I would quit also. We did get the support from many other Bruce's students in

Hollywood like Steve McQueen to keep perpetuating Bruce's message and ideas.

At that time, we had a group of students that were training in Dan's backyard. After a couple of months, Dan called me up and said, "Let's open a school together. There are a lot of people who want to learn Bruce Lee's method". Everything changed then. We both felt it was up to us to keep his legacy alive so we became partners and opened the old "Filipino Kali Academy" in Torrance, California in 1974. We had two reasons for opening the Filipino Kali Academy, one was to share Bruce's philosophy and arts and two was to revive and promote the Filipino Martial Arts.

How has the teaching changed from the old Kali Academy to the new schools?

This is a very interesting question. At the Kali Academy the students used to spar very often and very hard. It was a testing ground. A lot of people left because of the hard sparring. It wasn't difficult to spot bruised shins, fat lips, black eyes, swollen forearms and thighs in the students. Sparring was the butter and bread. It was very a diehard mentality. Nowadays, circumstances have changed. Of course we do spar, but the mentality is different. We drill much more than before. People want to enjoy the training and don't want to be hurt all the time. They want to be in good shape and physical condition – their goal is not to be fighters. Definitely, there are still some diehards and these have to be trained in a very different way. Personally, I like to teach everything. I don't hold anything back. I'm not doing my job unless my students can eventually kick my butt!"

How the FMA training you received was different from the Bruce Lee approach?

For example, the majority of the Filipino Martial Art systems are designed around twelve lines or twelve angles of attack and you had to teach that first. They all have a counter defense to match. Once you understand the concepts and philosophy of the style, you can develop your own creation by combining patterns of motion. It's like dancing; once you can do the foxtrot or waltz and their movement and rhythms then perhaps you can create your own dance. The real difference in the Filipino Martial Arts and Bruce Lee's JKD is for each individual. The individual is more important than any style or system. Throughout many years of intensive training with some incredible instructors – the Filipino arts teaches you that you can't do a passive block or you'll get hurt because a the combination of strikes that

ESCRIMA MASTERS

will follow. We have learned that blocks need to become strikes. Bruce in JKD wanted us to intercept. Thus an attack become the defense.

Does the edged weapon require different training than empty hands?

Yes they do but edge weapons and blunt impact weapons are similar and transferable. Edge weapons have a special application because of a sharp point and edge. To be proficient in edge weapons, requires learnt very specific skills. Blunt impact weapons are normally power strikes with minimum skills required. Formal training in impact weapons and edge weapons will give one the benefit to transpose one weapon to the other but you need to know how to do it.

What are the similarities and differences between Panantukan or Filipino boxing and Western boxing?

Both, Panantukan and Western boxing, are hand-striking arts. Boxing, however, is limited to punching or the Pugilistic art. The Filipino art of Panantukan is the art of striking with an open hand or closed fist and includes the use of the elbow both for defense and attack. There are many aspects that can be considered "dirty" in Western Boxing but that are extremely effective for real combat.

What does the IMB logo symbolize?

The logo represents a trilogy philosophy of: black/gray/white, heavy/middle/light, hard/firm/soft, long/medium/short, and offense/defense/counter. It also expresses the three combative ranges: the long range weaponry of escrima/kali/arnis; the middle-range strikes of boxing/Muay Thai; and the close-range grappling of wrestling/jiu-jitsu/judo. We provide the student with the three basic ranges of various martial art disciplines. They practice them on their own and they make their own decision on what best fits their needs. We don't want to teach them only martial arts. We want them to be able to develop it. This is ultimately IMB's goal.

What is the program that you use at the IMB for the Filipino Arts?

The program that I use at IMB Academy consists of the fundamental basic coordination and exercises for angling, footwork for defense, offence and counter techniques. The intermediate stage continues with the lines of attack for the numbering system of many different style including disarming techniques. Later on "Pormas" or forms are added to enhance weapon control and handling. Advance stage

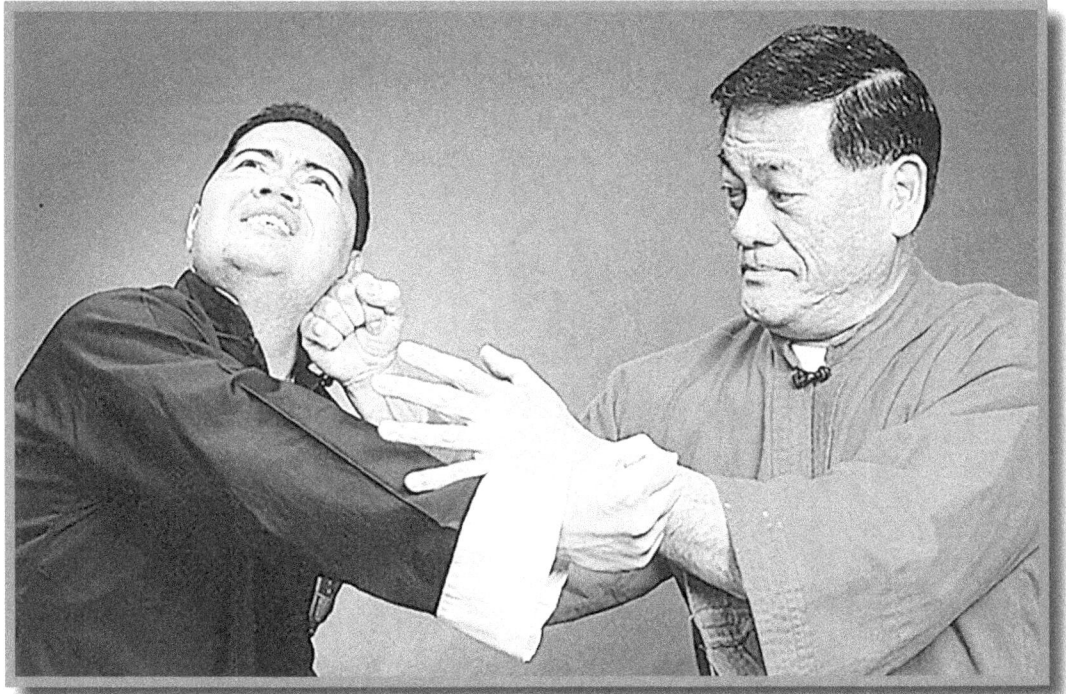

is the sparring training of single or double weapons. Weapons against empty hand sparring is also introduced at this level but requires a higher level of training.

What motivates you to keep going forward?

The challenges of every new day motivate me to do better today than yesterday. That's how I see life. I surround myself with what I love, whether it is family, friends, students, music, hobbies, home, and whatever makes me happy and productive. The spirit of Bruce lee continues to be an inspiration in my life. There isn't a day that goes by that I don't think of him and the friends and teachers that made my life possible.

If there is one most important thing you could pass on to the practitioners, what would it be?

Attitude is clearly number one for me. I have seen very talented martial artist who have a poor attitude. It is easy to acquire skills. However, it is difficult to recognize ones own enduring attitude. I believe respect is earned. The more you give, the more you get back. One should develop an attitude of gratitude. One should give thanks for everything that happened to oneself, knowing that every step forward is a step toward achieving something bigger and better than before. For me the Budo Code is the main thing. I have followed the powerful and uncompromising Budo Code for almost all my life. In accordance with the Code, I have been teaching one of the highest skills of humankind: how to gain self-confidence and increased self-respect.

CACOY CANETE

THE ESKRIMA LEGEND

Circa Cañete, or "Cacoy," as he is known by his Filipino nickname, was born in the Visayas region of the Philippines. Some of the styles he has learned include Ju Jitsu, Boxing, Kodokan Judo, free style wrestling, Shorin Karate, and Aikido. With his acknowledged spectrum of skills through his lifetime of training, he has gained deep insight and broad understanding, with mastery of the concepts of self-defense and combat. The culmination of years of learning fused into the style that he teaches, which is called "Eskrido." This style combines the refined essential elements of every martial art he has learned through his life. "Cacoy" Canete is the last surviving member and the only 12th degree black belt and the highest ranking member of the fame Doce Pares Eskrima Club.

How long have you been practicing martial arts?

First of all, I would like to state that I belong to a family of twelve siblings. Born in San Fernando, Cebu in 1919, I'm the youngest of the siblings, eight brothers and four sisters, who had an obsession to practice eskrima, the Filipino Martial Arts. My father and his two brothers also were eskrimadors. Likewise, my mother's brother was an eskrimador. We all grew up in Cebu City, Philippines.

Our martial art organization, popularly known as Doce Pares, was founded in Cebu City in 1932. The 24 founding masters were led by Lorenzo Saavedra, nephews Teodoro and Federico Saavedra, and brothers Eulgio Cañete and Felimon Cañete. Euolgio Cañete was elected first president of the organization and remained in that position until his death in 1988, at age 87. As my brother's successor, I have been president of Docer Pares from 1988 to the present. In 1996, Doce Pares was renamed Doce Pares World Federation. But in late 2001, Doce Pares was changed to Cacoy Doce Pares World Federation. Doce Pares is a Spanish term, which means 12 pairs. This term is significant because it refers to 12 pairs of eskrima masters, 12 basic strikes, and 12 counter strikes; coincidentally, we were 12 siblings in the family.

ESCRIMA MASTERS

My mentor in martial arts was my older brother Felimon "Momoy" Cañete, who taught me boxing when I was 5 years old and also eskrima a couple of years later. To sum up, I have been in the practice of eskrima for 82 years now.

What were the teaching methods like?

My older brother Momoy chose to have my training of martial arts at home. He really wanted it very personal and private. In his method of teaching, he always emphasized the basics. He truly was a teacher who kept stressing discipline during workouts. Regular drills for proficiency in stick and dagger eskrima had been done for many years. It wasn't until 1949 that my training shifted to single stick eskrima. That tells you how important the aspects of stick and dagger is in Doce Pares Eskrima.

Do you have a particularly memorable experience?

I have many. Just think of all these years of training, fighting, and teaching. My teacher, elder brother Felimon Cañete, was a perfectionist and disciplinarian. Every now and then, he would tell me to observe strictly the schedule on regular training in martial arts. Although he was a very practical man, he always thought that etiquette and good manners are very important for the martial artists, regardless of the style they practice.

How has your perception of the art and training in eskrima developed over the years?

Just watching the eskrima masters inmerse themselves in training inspired me to work long and hard in the martial arts, so much so that I was able to revolutionize eskrima in 1949. I did it because I felt it was necessary to incorporate certain elements that should be part of the style.

Do you think there is still a "pure" system of kali and eskrima, or we are going to a more "mixed" approach?

With the unstoppable growth and popularity of martial arts in the Philippines such as jujitsu, judo, aikido, karate, wrestling, boxing, and other Asian arts, it is certain the system of kali, eskrima and arnis eventually will take the mixed approach. I don't think this is good or bad, but I believe we should maintain a certain clarity of what is what and the differences between one style of martial art and another.

What are the major changes in the arts since you began training?

My knowledge in other martial arts systems such as boxing, jujitsu, aikido, wrestling, karate, and kung fu has enabled me to take steps toward the development of Eskrido, the intigration of eskrima, jujitsu, judo and aikido.

How do you think a practitioner can increase his or her understanding of the spiritual aspects of the arts?

Meditation and abdominal breathing exercises usually are done among senior instructors and masters in martial arts, regardless of the style. Such practice leads to peace of mind, relaxation, and energizing of one's body before going into long and hard workouts in eskrima and other martial arts. Eventually, when all actions and reactions become automatic, it shows that the body, mind, and spirit are in harmony. And this is the highest technical level any martial artist can aim for.

Do you think that the technical level of the Filipino Arts in the West has caught up to the level of the Philippines?

For having fulfilled commitment to develop and propagate eskrima in North America and Europe, no doubt eskrima in the West has caught up to the level of the Philippines. I am sure about this. There are great eskrimadors all over the world. Phillipines is still the motherland of the art but the technical level is very high all around the globe.

ESCRIMA MASTERS

Are martial arts a sport or a way of life?

Eskrima, being practiced for self-defense as well as for as a sport, promotes brotherhood. As a way of life, it promotes physical, mental, and spiritual well being. I think we should keep an open mind and use the art for different purposes. Eskrima is not only one thing. It is what we want to make of it.

Do you think it helps students to train with weapons?

Eskrima students who have the knowledge of other martial arts are trained not only to defend themselves against bare hands, feet, and stick attack but also against deadly weapons like knives and swords or machetes. I truly think any martial artist, regardless of style, should learn how to defend him or herself against these type of weapons. You never know…

Who would you like to have trained with that you have not and why?

When I was young, I had wished to get special instructions from other top eskrima masters. Unluckily, it did not happen. They all were busy with their students…but to be honest, I did train under some of the best eskrimadors in history, so I am not sure how much I did miss.

What keeps you motivated to train after all these years?

In my more than 20 years of travel to many countries all over the world to conduct eskrima seminars and workshops, I have observed that the people enthusiastically welcome the Doce Pares style. In view of this, I have resolved to keep myself busy in the practice of eskrima, without thinking of retirement. Besides, regular workouts keep me healthy in mind and body. My motivation lies in the love I have for the art.

Do you think no-holds-barred (MMA) events bring positive or negative aspects to the martial arts?

People getting involved actively in no-holds-barred have developed self-confidence and discipline to do that, and if it is good for them, that is fine for them. But that is not for everybody and these approaches are not what the true martial arts are all about.

What are your thoughts on the future of Filipino Martial arts?

I have found that practitioners around the world have accepted eskrima as a sport and as a way of life. For this reason, I can state positively that there is a bright future for the Filipino martial arts.

Do you have any general advice to pass on?

My advice to people who have keen interest in the study of eskrima is to keep practicing the art with dedication. There is a saying that practice makes perfect. So never stop practicing, no matter what. The true value of martial arts lies in its morals and philosophy.

VIRGIL CAVADA

INTO THE BLADE

Founder and Headmaster of Applied Eskrima, Master Virgil Orlanes Cavada was born in Cebu, Philippines in 1954. He began studying Karate at age 15. At age 17, he enrolled at the University of San Jose Recoletos in Cebu, where he studied Mechanical Engineering and competed in collegiate weightlifting competitions. Eventually he was named captain of the team and was nominated to join the Philippine National team for the Asian Games. Virgil competed for 6 years.

At age 19, he was recruited to join an Eskrima group headed by Vicente Atillo and his son Crispulo. Vicente Atillo was a well-known weightlifter and wrestler in Cebu.

As true in most of his endeavors, it was not long before Virgil distinguished himself in Eskrima. In March of 1976, he became Grandmaster Crispulo Atillo's primary sparring and training partner at the first Asian Martial Arts Festival.

Virgil Cavada also appeared on the first instructional DVD release of the "Atillo Balintawak" Saavedra Style in January of 2010. Since then, the system has been accepted by followers of other Filipino Styles wishing to augment their training with the devastatingly effective methods of the "Balintawak" style. Even martial arts legends like Guro Dan Inosanto have been learning the style. Guro Dan has been gradually introducing the style at his seminars all over the world, and when his schedule permits, he continues to study with Master Cavada.

How long have you been practicing Filipino martial arts and who were your teachers?

I was introduced to Eskrima when I was in college studying in Mechanical Engineering in 1973. I was then a member of the collegiate weightlifting team and one of my teammate was the neighbor of a family that trains in Eskrima/Arnis. I will always be grateful to Victorino Tabar for introducing me to the Atillo family in Cebu, Philippines.

ESCRIMA MASTERS

I have only two teachers and that is the father, GM Vicente Atillo, known as Noy Inting and his son, GM Crispulo Atillo, known as Noy Ising.

How many styles (Eskrima or other methods) have you trained on?

My foundation in based solely on the Balintawak based Eskrima coming from my two teachers. However, before learning Eskrima in 1973, I have two years of Karate (mostly katas of course) and two years experience in collegiate weightlifting competitions. Applied Eskrima also adopts the positives of the long-range system because I totally believe the person who knows how to move in and out during a fight has a big advantage. I teach students close quarters Eskrima/Arnis, but also teaches them how to fight in long range, and then be able to go from long range to close range and from close range to long range. In life and death situations, we should not have any limitations in movements and we must be able or have the knowledge and ability to use any means necessary to survive. I owe a deep gratitude to my two teachers for teaching me selflessly the art of Eskrima/Arnis. That knowledge is what I used to start Applied Eskrima and over the years, Applied Eskrima has totally evolve and expanded to where it is today, a totally different system from what I learned in 1973.

Would you tell us some interesting stories of your early days in Eskrima?

Training in Eskrima in the 1970's was bare bone. Meaning, you come as is, and training was tough. We do not have safety gears like we have now, like head gears, shin guards, hand gloves, eye goggles, etc.......

We also train outside under a tree and benches are on the side for onlookers and other students to sit and watch. When it is rainy season, we wait for a downpour to stop and find a ground that is not soggy and train from that area. We might not have the luxury of a gym during that time, but it was what we had and it was an experience I will never forget. The bonding with other students and with your teachers was great. You treat each other as part of your extended family. Of course, training without laughter is no fun, because jokes are part of Eskrima/Arnis training.

Were you 'natural' at Eskrima – did the movements come easily to you ?

Growing up in a town 57 kilometers or 35.6 miles North of Cebu City, Philippines, I was always outside during the day, playing with other kids, swimming anytime at sea where it was just about 500 feet from my house or climbing at fruit trees or in the afternoon playing war games based on Western movies we saw the night before at the town plaza for free! So yes, the movements of Eskrima were easy to absorb since my body was prepared by movements in my younger days. The fast movements of the sticks took a little while to adjust.

How has your personal expression of Eskrima has developed over the years?

Each person is built differently physically and mentally from the next person and so on. Eventually in the progression of learning any martial arts, we tend to develop our very own way of expressing a movement, of showing and accomplishing a certain technique. My personal journey in Eskrima/Arnis is continuing and I am still seeking improvement from all areas. I also have to be careful not to get injured because injuries always set our training backwards and even when healed our movements are not the same. I always emphasize to students the proper control when doing fast sparring or executing any technique specially if speed is involve. If he/she do not know how to control or know when to stop, most likely someone will get injured. We train as close to a realistic scenario as much as possible, but with emphasis on safety first.

Do you think different 'styles' are truly important in the art of Eskrima/Kali? Why?

Of course, It is very important to have different 'styles' in the art of Eskrima/Arnis/Kali. Filipino Martial Arts is composed of so many styles and each one has a very unique contribution in the development of the art. For instance, a certain style blocks a direct strike to the head with the stick on a horizontal position, while another style will block the same attack with the stick in a diagonal position, and another style blocks the same strike to the head area with the butt of the stick in an upward position. Other styles will turn their body sideways to defend themselves and others will step back, some will just

ESCRIMA MASTERS

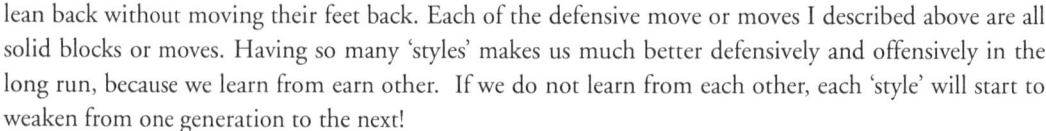

lean back without moving their feet back. Each of the defensive move or moves I described above are all solid blocks or moves. Having so many 'styles' makes us much better defensively and offensively in the long run, because we learn from earn other. If we do not learn from each other, each 'style' will start to weaken from one generation to the next!

What do you remember the most of all the masters you had the opportunity of training with?

I have not trained directly with any other masters, but I have meet and interacted with so many known masters and grandmasters within the Filipino Martial Arts community and other martial arts systems over the years. One thing certain on all of them is that they carry that aura of positive energy and respect. Specially respect to everyone in general and being humble. For me, respect is a two way street. If you demand respect, it will be given to you but after awhile it will wear out and that respect will vanish because it was not earned. Respect must be earned and must be mutual!

Please tell us a little bit about the philosophical and spiritual aspects of your system?

I formed Applied Eskrima with one major goal in mind and that is to develop a practitioners reflex speed. I totally believe that once a person has a decent reflex speed he can easily defend and attack and has a bigger chance of surviving a realistic attack. At the very beginning of learning, students are told how stick movements can easily be interpreted into empty hands movements. It is not easy for most but the most important thing is that they understand that the stick is just a tool for developing the reflex speed specially with the non-dominant hand. If in the course of a fight, you get hold of any weapon or object your reflex/body will not have to think once on how to use it or what to do with it. I also believe that training the mind as well as the body because we need both to be strong and healthy to be able to function fully at our peak when we have to defend ourselves or our love ones! Applied Eskrima has a total of 10 Modules to study. Each module has at least 25 lessons each. The very first Module is the Basics Module and teaches drills and techniques necessary for learning the more advance lessons. Developing ones reflex speed allows that person to survive an actual scenario with little technical knowledge or knowhow. I am also very strict on the forms specially beginners, because majority just want to learn advance lessons without seriously concentrating on the forms. I always say, Forms first before Speed. Sometimes, I say, Forms first before speed and power, etc…..

How different from other Martial Arts styles do you see the principles and concepts of Eskrima?

By now almost everyone knows that Eskrima/Arnis start their student learning by introducing the weapon first. Majority of the systems start with the stick, a few start with the knife or bolo.

The use of the weapon while training the new student is the biggest difference from other martial arts styles. After that the techniques, movements and drills are focused towards an opponent holding a weapon, blunt or bladed. The corresponding movements of the practitioner will be different from a style that does not teach how to deal with weapons because any type of blunt or bladed weapons are more life threatening than purely empty hands styles. Even the empty hands applications movements and techniques of Eskrima/Arnis are unconventional, to say the least.

Do you think that Eskrima in the West has 'caught up' with the technical level in the Philippines?

I would say, about equal or even because foreign based Filipinos who teaches Eskrima/Arnis are many and they are very highly knowledgeable and they produce great students and instructors as well! Likewise, Philippines based teachers are many and equally highly knowledgeable in teaching the arts. In the long term, It is not a question of whether the technical level of Eskrima/Arnis of the West has caught up with the technical level in the Philippines. It is a question of a personal level. It is how each one of us, from any country in the world concentrates on learning and improving in the Filipino Martial Arts of Eskrima/Arnis! The quality of teaching and knowledge being offered in the Philippines and in the West are practically the same or equal. It is therefore, up to the individual practitioner to excel as far as his/her mind and body allows him/her to achieve!

Eskrima and Arnis is nowadays often referred to as a sport... would you agree with this definition?

Yes and No. Yes, I agree that it is referred to as a sport because of the tournament side of Eskrima/Arnis. All martial arts tournaments have rules and most rules are there to protect the participants from serious injuries. Tournaments also contributed so much to the rise and popularity of Eskrima/Arnis around the world. The flip side is that most people think all systems or styles of Eskrima/Arnis are mostly the same, just for tournament preparations. No, I do not agree because majority of people do not know that even systems/styles that are geared for tournaments have their own realistic or street sce-

narios training and techniques and that the tournaments are just to test certain attributes of the art, like conditioning, footwork, distance and timing...Not counting the publicity or marketing side of the events.

Do you feel that you still have further to go in your studies of the art?

Personally, I feel this Filipino Martial Arts journey is a lifetime endeavor. Our learning has to be continuous in order to improve year after year. For serious practitioners: You do not want to attain a certain expertise or level and then totally stop and expect that knowledge to be at top level years after you stop training! The more you teach, the more you learn and the more you learn the more you can teach! For me learning in martial arts and life in general is a daily experience and will only stop when I cannot physically move anymore. I am still learning and improving daily. I always ask myself the question of, What If? That is why I teach students how to keep distance and how to close the distance, because staying in one area is not wise and safe and advantageous.

Do you have any general advice you would care to pass on the practitioners in general?

Being good or being an expert in martial arts in general is not easy, but not impossible. It requires the same focus and dedication like any other endeavors in life. If you really want to achieve a certain degree of knowledge, you have to work on learning how and the steps of achieving it and then spare enough allowable time to train.

There are no secrets in being good in martial arts! Training on the correct moves or drills or techniques for hours and hours, a thousand times a thousand hours is the key. With so many distractions in our modern society, you must budget enough time for your training. If you put in very little time for training, you must not expect amazing results in a short time. You are how you train!

Some people think going to the Philippines to really progress in the art is highly necessary, do you share this point of view?

Visiting the Philippines is highly recommended but it all depends on the time and budget of the practitioner. Visiting the country of origin of the martial arts that you are passionate about will elevate your desire for more knowledge, will make you appreciate the culture of that country, will give you more insights of the background of your teacher, will give you a clearer picture when your teacher describes places, events and situations of that country. Overall, visiting the Philippines will not only elevate your physical learning, it will also enrich you mentally by absorbing a different culture! I always encourage every Filipino Martial Arts practitioner to visit The Philippines if their time and budget allow them!

What are your thoughts on the future of the art?

Filipino Martial Arts in general still has a long way to go to be fully recognized as part of the main stream, but the direction where it is headed in the last 10 years is in the right direction! Even today, most people still cannot separate the stick from the empty hands. Meaning: When you mention Eskrima/Arnis, they always assume that you cannot move or fight without a stick on your hand.

It is the job of all teachers of Filipino Martial Arts that at the very beginning of learning, the students must totally understand that we can fight with or without using the stick or knife! The stick or knife or bolo is just an extension of our hands. We, as teachers must repeat that again and again for all to absorb and totally understand.

The next 10 years is looking very bright and hopeful for Eskrima/Arnis around the world. The hard work that Filipino Martial Arts forefathers started long time ago and continued by numerous teachers today is finally showing signs of blooming. As long as respect and cooperation are in the agenda and the crab mentality put aside or totally squashed, nothing will stop Eskrima/Arnis from reaching its long awaited and much deserved glory within the martial arts world! Mabuhay ! Mabuhay ang Pilipinas !! Mabuhay ang Pilipino !!!

LEO M. GIRON

THE LAST OF THE BLADED WARRIORS

GRAND MASTER EMERITUS LEO GIRON WAS BORN IN BAYAMBANG, PHILLIPINES, IN THE PROVINCE OF PANGASINAN. HE WAS A WORLD WAR II VETERAN WHO WAS AWARDED THE BRONZE STAR, AMONG MANY OTHER CITATIONS FOR HEROISM. AS THE HEAD ADVISOR AND FOUNDER OF THE BAHALA NA MARTIAL ARTS ASSOCIATION, HE WAS WORLD RENOWNED AS THE FATHER OF LARGA MANO IN AMERICA. SOME OF GIRON'S MOST NOTED DISCIPLES ARE DAN INOSANTO, RICHARD BUSTILLO, TED LUCAYLUCAY, JERRY POTEET, AND DENTOY RIVELLAR. GIRON WAS STILL ACTIVE AND TEACHING UNTIL HIS FINAL DAYS, ALONG WITH GRANDMASTER ANTONIO E. SOMERA, AT THEIR HOME SCHOOL IN STOCKTON, CALIFORNIA. AT THE TENDER AGE OF 90 HE STILL ATTENDED CLASS ON A REGULAR BASES. HIS KNOWLEDGE OF JUNGLE WARFARE WAS AN INVALUABLE ASSET TO THOSE THAT TRAIN WITH HIM AND SEEK KNOWLEDGE OF "REAL" COMBAT. HIS APPEARANCE WAS THAT OF A HUMBLE MAN, AND HE CARRIED HIMSELF WITH THE DEMEANOR OF A DISTINGUISHED COLLEGE PROFESSOR. HOWEVER, THERE WAS A UNMISTAKABLE SERIOUSNESS ABOUT HIM AND A HINT OF THE FIST THAT LIES WITHIN THE VELVET GLOVE — PERHAPS SOMETHING YOU ONLY GET WHEN YOU FIGHT AGAINST MEN WHO WOULD TAKE YOUR LIFE AWAY.

When were you inducted into the Army?

I was inducted on October 9, 1942, in Los Angeles, California. Prior to that I was farming in Imperial Valley, California. I was first stationed at Camp San Luis Obispo and then in the winter of the same year I was transferred to Fort Ord.

How were you selected to be in the 978th Signal Service company?

Well, everyone was brought into the base recreation room and given an aptitude test. Many did not pass and were sent back to their regiments. Others made it and were given additional education in

ESCRIMA MASTERS

Morse code. The Army was looking for specific types of men. They were looking for men with schooling who could communicate well in English. I was one of the few that made it.

What was your training like in the Army?

During boot camp we also went to school. We were learning communications like Morse code, wig-wag (flag signals), cyma four, cryptography and paraphrasing. I was trained to communicate. At the time I did not know what the Army was planning for me. We were never told why we were training; we just did what the Army told us to do.

What type of self-defense training did you receive from the Army?

We learned all the basic training needed for soldiering. Nothing special – just how to shoot a carbine, how to use a .45 and some basic hand-to-hand combat. I was fortunate to learn escrima as a child and later on, after coming to America, from one of my most influential teachers, Flaviano Vergara. Flaviano is the man who taught me the most about escrima and how to defend myself. In fact I met Flaviano a second time in Fort Ord during which time we would play on weekdays after dinner, and on the weekends while everyone else went to town. Flaviano and I would do nothing but drill and drill using estilo de fondo and larga mano. Sometimes a soldier would come by and ask what were we doing? Some would tell us that they would never come close to a samurai sword. They claimed they would give the samurai a load of their M-1.

What were you first experiences with the art of escrima?

As a kid, every time my friends and I heard the "click, click, click" of knives, we would be playing under the mango trees and the trail would be guarded. So I would sneak away to watch. Later, we paid so many bundles of straw and rice for our lessons. My family didn't know. I was carrying a bundle or rice when my father asked me about it and I told him I was going to take it to my uncle; we were going to make cakes!

In one of my first training sessions my instructor told me, "Take you bolo and let's do some training. Don't worry about hurting me because I've been fighting for a long time. Cut me anytime you can. If you touch me you'll get a month's pay." That was the way you learned in those days. I learned a lot about how to use the environment for survival purposes. This is a very important aspect, especially when you're fighting in the jungle. You need to know how to maximize every tree and every bush – the smallest advantage may be what you need to save your life.

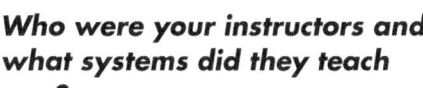

GIRON

Who were your instructors and what systems did they teach you?

I had five teachers and I will give them to you in order and what style they passed onto me.

1. **Benito Junio** from the barrio of Inerangan town of Bayombang province of Pangasinan, Luzon Philippines. In 1920 I started my education in arnis escrima. Benito Junio was famous for his larga mano (long-hand stick) and fondo fuerte (fighting in a solid position) styles.

2. **Fructuso Junio** from the barrio of Telbang town of Bayombang provice of Pangasinan, Luzon Philippines. From 1921-1926 I continued my training with Fructuso uncle to Bentio. Fructuso Junio was well-known for his macabebe or two-stick fighting. Fructuso was the first to share the importance of distinguishing between the old (cada-anan) and new (cabaroan) styles of Luzon.

3. **Flavian Vergara** from Santa Curz in Llocos Sur Luzon, Philippines. Vergara was the top student of Dalmacio Bergonia who defeated the great champion Santiago Toledo. Vergara and I started our training in the prune orchards of Meridian, California from 1929-1932. Vergara and Giron would meet again directly after the outbreak of World War II. Our lives would cross for the last time in October 1942, when I was shipped out to Fort Ord, Calif. Every spare minute Vergara and I would train until I was shipped out in January, 1943. Vergara was a master in the Bergonia style and very proficient in the estilo elastico (rubber band style). I always thought that Vergara had superhuman abilities. Vergara influenced me a lot and his understanding of the relationships between the cada-anan and cabaroan styles of arnis escrima.

4. **Beningo Ramos** from Kongkong Bayongbang. During World War II Ramos was a sergeant in the Filipino army assigned to me. Pryor to the outbreak of World War II Ramos was an improbable arnis escrima teacher and was respected as one of the best estilo matador (killer-style) teachers in Luzon. Ramos was an expert in larga mano, miscla contras, tero pisada, tero grave and elastico styles. Ramos was so confident of his skills that he and I would play with live bolos. Ramos bet me that if I could hit him he would give me one month's pay. I never collected a cent from Ramos.

5. **Julian Bundoc** from the barrio of Carangay town of Bayombang province of Pangasianan, Luzon Philippines. Julian was cousin to Benito Junio. Julian Bundoc and I would play more of the combative larga mano and work on conditioning the body. Julian Bundoc was also a master of hilot or massage. We trained in Stockton from 1956-1961. One of my teachers named Flaviano Vergara had the most influence on me and helped me greatly in developing my system.

ESCRIMA MASTERS

How many systems or methods comprise your own personal method?

I'm well-known around the world for my larga mano style of escrima. But this is just a small piece of the entire Giron arnis escrima system. The Giron system has 20 styles and techniques that are just as effective and just as complete. Here are the names and a brief overview of each of the 20 styles (estilo) that encompass my method:

1. **Estilo de Fondo** – This is a style of planting yourself firmly on the ground. During combat you do not want to move your feet about, as this may cause you to lose your footing and balance. This style counters off the 12 angles of attack using a 24-inch stick which simulates the bolo. There are approximately 160 counter movements in this style.

2. **Estilo de Abanico** – This is a fanning style encompassing the use of the side of the weapon (stick or blade) to block oncoming attacks. Counterstriking is included, with the emphasis on the tip of your weapon to get the maximum amount of power in short and powerful striking ranges.

3. **Estilo Abierta** – This style refers to an open body style of fighting. This style is used by the most advanced students to calculate the distance between themselves and their opponent. The student will calculate the opponent's strikes and will open his body position and counterstrike within the same motion, leaving the opponent with little or no counter.

4. **Estilo de Salon** – This is a dance-like style. This style uses fast and solid footwork that also involves the use of stick work.

5. E**stilo Sonkete** — This is the style of poking and thrusting. As your opponent attacks you can use the components of parrying, blocking, evading, and deflection while applying the counterthrust or poke into the opponent's guard.

6. **Estilo Retirada** — This is a style of retreating used to draw your opponent in or to create an opening in the opponent's defense. Once this has taken place you can use counterstriking to render your opponent helpless. Retreating footwork, evading, and counterstriking is the key.

7. **Estilo Elastico** — An elastic or rubber-band style. It makes use of one's stretching ability to reach a given target. This style is a necessity that is woven into the larga mano (long hand) style. Many feel that the person who plays estilo elastico possesses superhuman ability and is difficult to defeat.

8. **Fondo Fuerte** — The escrimador's last stand. You must plant yourself effectively into a reliable spot where you can revolve to meet an opponent's attacks without losing ground.

9. **Contra Compas** — These Spanish words mean "against time." In terms of Giron arnis escrima this is a style of striking with off-beat timing or broken rhythm.

10. **Estlio Redonda** — This is a round or circular style of fighting. To be effective in this style you must be able to maneuver your strikes in circular movements horizontally, vertically, and diagonally, from both high and low positions.

11. **Combate Adentro** — This style is used to ward off opponents using paired weapons, such as the sword and dagger. With this style, you defend yourself inside the opponent's circle using solid footwork and slicing counterstrikes.

12. **Tero Grave** — This style implies the use of serious or deadly strikes to critical areas of the body.

13. **Estilo Macabebe** — Macabebe is the name of a town in the province of Pampanga, Philippines. These fierce warriors are famous for the use of two weapons or two sticks. This style is characterized by the interweaving motions of the weapons and is also known as sinawali.

14. **Tero Pisada** — This style incorporates the use of double or two-handed striking and blocking. The blocking is so intense that it will paralyze the opponent's hands and will create an opening for your two-handed counterstrike.

15. **Media Media** — The term "media media" implies "half of half." In terms of fighting, the concept refers to fighting at half-range and striking on half-timing.

16. **Cadena de Mano** — This is a hand-to-hand combat method which uses parrying, grabbing, twisting, locking, and chocking in succession. In other words, you chain the hand movements together from close quarters.

17. **Escape** — This style stresses evasion and methods of warding off the opponent's attacks.

18. **Estilo Bolante** — This style is named after a person named Braulio Bolante from Dagupan, Pagasinan, Philippines. This style uses vertical striking patterns and is an excellent method of fighting in doorways and narrow passages.

19. **Miscla (Mezcla) Contras** — This style favors defending yourself against multiple opponents and multiple attacks. It stresses placing oneself in the proper place and position in relation to the opponent.

ESCRIMA MASTERS

20. **Largo mano** — This style maintains long-distance fighting without jeopardizing safety. The counter concept is centered on attacking the closest target of your opponent, and terminating the contest with the first counter-strike.

When did you go overseas for the Army?

On December 10, 1943, two of us were shipped to New Guinea but this was a mistake by the Army as we were suppose to go to Australia. So on January 10, 1944, I was sent to Australia to a place called Camp X. It was close to the little town of Beau Desert about 60 miles from the seaport of Brisbane in Queensland. It was there that I furthered my training in Morse code, cryptography, visual communications, et cetera. I also embarked on my final training in jungle warfare in a place called Canungra. Thirteen weeks of hard training contributed to my ability to climb the high mountains of the Philippines and surviving in it's jungles jungles. At one time, for a week's period, we were given only three days of sea rations and the other four days we had to survive on our own. At this point I was a staff sergeant.

Did you ever meet General Douglas MacArthur?

Yes, several times. But on August 10, 1944 I was ordered to a briefing at the General's headquarters. General MacArthur crossed his arms and said to us, "Boys, I selected you to do a job that a general can't do. You have the training to do a job that no one else can. You are going home to our country, the Philippines – yours and my homeland. You'll serve as my eyes, my ears, and my fingers, and you'll keep me informed of what the enemy is doing. You will tell me how to win the war by furnishing me with this information, which I could not obtain in any other way. Good luck, and there will be shinning bars waiting for you in Manila."

How did you landed in the Philippines?

On August 12, 1944 we boarded one of the smallest submarines in the United States Navy armada – the U.S. Sting Ray. We were loaded and armed with carbines, submachine guns, side arms, bolo knives, trench knives, brass knuckles, ammunition and a few other special packages. While on our way to the Philippines we slept on our own cargo boxes. Myself and one other soldier slept under the torpedo racks. There was one time when we were fired upon and had to out-maneuver several torpedoes at full speed. This occurred near the Halmahera Island on the Celebes Sea. One other time when we were attack was in Caonayan Bay just before disembarking the submarine. The attack occurred when a Japanese warplane dropped depth charges on us. They came close enough to rattle the sub and burst some pipes but luckily this was the extent of the damage. We landed on the beach on August 28, 1944.

What was the most memorable encounter you had with the enemy?

Well, it is hard to try to choose one particular encounter because they were all very horrifying. One bonsai attack particularly comes to mind. In early June, 1945, on a rainy day, an enemy platoon detected us and charged our position. We formed in a wedge or triangle formation, two on the side and one point man in front – me. Just like any bonsai charge the enemy was very noisy. Yelling and shouting, they were not afraid to die. The Filipino guerrillas, on the other hand, would chew their tobacco, grit their teeth, and swing their bolos in deadly and eerie silence. They would chop here and jab there with long bolos, short daggers, and pointed bamboo. They pulverized chili peppers with sand and deposited the mixture in bamboo tubes to spray the enemies' eyes, so they couldn't see. As the enemy closed, my adrenaline shot up and a bayonet and a samurai sword came at me simultaneously. The samurai sword was in front of me while the bayonet was little to the left. With my left hand I parried the bayonet and with my stick I blocked the sword coming down on me. The bayonet man went by and his body came in line with my bolo, so I slashed down and cut his left hip. The samurai came back with a backhand blow and I met his tricep with the bolo, chopping it to the ground.

After the encounter I wiped my face with my left hand to clear my eyes from the rain and found bloodstains on my face. The blood had come from my hand. I had felt the twitch on the meaty part of my left palm when I parried the bayonet, but I didn't know that I had been cut. There were many more encounters but we were not there to fight. Our job was to not be detected by the enemy and to send back vital information about trooop movements and strength to headquarters.

When did you start teaching the art of arnis escrima?

In October, 1968 I decided to open a club in Tracy, California, where I was residing at the time. I was motivated after I heard on the news that a man in Chicago killed eight nursing students and some of the nurses were Filipinas. I wanted to teach people to defend themselves against senseless violence.

ESCRIMA MASTERS

Why did you name your martial art association "Bahala Na?"

It was the slogan of my outfit during World War II. I am proud of the men I fought with during World War II and of the spirit of my fallen comrades; I hold the memories of all of those I fought with in very high regard and close to my heart. I also can associate the combative spirit we had during the time of World War II with our training. Because of this I feel I have the right to use the slogan of "Bahala Na." It means "Come What May."

What makes a good student?

A person with good passive resistance. You must have patience and not be to eager to win and be the champion. What the student should be interested in, is to learn how to defend themselves and their family against aggression. The end result will be that you will survive, and this makes you victorious. You do not need to say, "I am going to win and defeat my opponent." The correct attitude is to say, "I am going to survive and not get hurt." That's what counts. If you hold your discipline and your style during the battle, the other man will eventually make a mistake, fall into a loophole, and give you an opening – he will defeat himself.

Did your experience during World War II help you to become a better teacher?

I know the respect of the bolo knife. Wartime is different. There is no regard for life. It's different teaching during peacetime – you must have structure and good communication with your students. I like to teach more about the application and fundamentals. It's not about how hard you hit or who is faster, its about sharing the art of our forefathers. Because if you analyze it, we are only the caretakers of the art for future generations.

Why do you still teach escrima?

Well, first of all, it's my hobby. I have the chance to stretch my legs, work my arms, and exercise my body. I feel it is a gift to be able to learn a combative art like escrima, and being that it falls in the field of sports it is good to have and know something that not many people know. I feel proud that I have something to share with the children of my friends and with those who want to learn an art that is different than other martial arts. I feel that the Filipino art is a superior art in comparison to other arts, so I stand firm in saying that I am proud that I have learned and know the art of escrima.

There have been reports of many escrima masters who have fought in death matches. Have you ever fought in a death match?

No, I have never fought in a death match. From what I understand, in order to participate in a death match you need to have a referee and a second – or a person in your corner similar to a boxing match. The only type of death match I had was during World War II. That was were I fought in the jungles for over a year, not knowing if I would survive from one day to the next. Our weapons of choice were the bolo knife or talonason – a long knife over was 36 inches long. There was no referee and no rules – the only rule was to survive.

What's your advice to martial arts practitioners today?

There seems to be an unstoppable, growing mentality of a need to fight and engage in combat in the current martial arts community. I fought for my life in a real war, and it is not glamorous or pleasant. Practitioners should focus on the general benefits of martial arts, from self-defense to using it as a way to achieve a better life, instead of trying to be a deadly fighting machine. We should strive to be better human beings – that should be the final goal of any martial art. Our goal should be to avoid fighting and to preserve life, not take enjoyment in hurting others and destroying life.

DAN INOSANTO

THE ETERNAL MASTER AND THE FOREVER STUDENT

HE IS THE MASTER EVERY STUDENT WANTS TO BE, AND THE STUDENT EVERY MASTER WOULD LIKE TO HAVE. ONE OF THE THREE MEN CHOSEN BY BRUCE LEE TO CARRY ON THE ART OF JEET KUNE DO, DAN INOSANTO WAS ORIGINALLY A KENPO KARATE STUDENT AND ED PARKER'S ASSISTANT INSTRUCTOR AND TOP BLACK BELT. INOSANTO MET BRUCE LEE IN 1964 AND HE BECAME HIS STUDENT AND PERSONAL TRAINING PARTNER AFTER A LONG CONVERSATION WHERE LEE EXPLAINED ART AND PHILOSOPHY TO DAN. APPOINTED BY BRUCE LEE AS THE INSTRUCTOR AT HIS LOS ANGELES, CHINATOWN KWOON, INOSANTO ALSO DID EXTENSIVE RESEARCH INTO THE FILIPINO MARTIAL ARTS, BECOMING ONE OF THE MOST OUTSTANDING FMA SCHOLARS AND INSTRUCTORS IN THE WORLD. INOSANTO'S MANY ACTIVITIES HAVE ALSO INCLUDED WRITING A VARIETY OF BOOKS ON JEET KUNE DO AND THE FILIPINO MARTIAL ARTS.

INOSANTO'S EVER-GROWING LEARNING DESIRE LED HIM TO STUDY UNDER THE MOST IMPORTANT TEACHER IN THE AMERICAN MARTIAL ARTS SCENE, INCLUDING ED PARKER, BRUCE LEE, ARK WONG, LEO GIRON, BEN LARGUSA, PAUL DE THOUARS, HERMAN SUWANDA, EDGAR SULITE, WALLY JAY, GENE LEBELL, AND MANY MORE. HE SEARCHED OUT AND STUDIED UNDER THE MOST FAMOUS MARTIAL ARTIST OF ALL TIME.

HIS PHILOSOPHY OF USING THE INSTRUCTOR'S WISDOM TO ACHIEVE FURTHER HEIGHTS IN THE MARTIAL ARTS IS WHAT MAKES DAN INOSANTO ONE OF A KIND, AND HIS ACADEMY THE MEETING POINT FOR PRACTITIONERS OF ALL STYLES FROM OVER THE WORLD. SIMPLY SAID, DANIEL A. INOSANTO IS THE MASTER EVERY STUDENT WANTS TO BE, AND THE STUDENT THAT EVERY MASTER WOULD LIKE TO HAVE.

Do you consider martial arts violent?

Many people look at the martial arts as a sign of violence. The goal of a good martial artist is to preserve life, not to destroy it. All the training in the world can't make you secure from every form of violence so the objective is to train the body to be able to preserve your life and the lives of your loved ones. Martial arts can bring people together and it is a very interesting way to educate ourselves about different cultures. Of course, the reason why you practice martial arts at 50 are different from what motivated you to begin training when you were 20.

Do you think there is a single "best" style?

I don't think so and I'll explain why. Some styles are efficient at a certain range of combat. Some look very impressive and you think right away they are devastating. Others don't look that impressive but they are very practical but you won't realize it until you're in the receiving end of one of their techniques. You have to find out if the style really fits your body type, which is very important. Some systems require a great deal of practice before you can effectively use them. Other styles can make you a very strong fighter in six months. In short, there isn't anything close to a "best style." You have to find what is best for you.

What kind of advise would you give to students?

I would recommend that if they have the time and the money, try and cross-train in as many styles as possible so you can get a deep understanding of different fighting forms and cultures.

Don't you think this can be very confusing for the student?

Don't misunderstand me. I don't mean the student has to jump from one system to another. First he needs what I call the "base" system. He needs years of training and understanding in this base system because it is from there that he will evolve. So he needs a strong foundation. This foundation is going to provide his building blocks.

You mentioned once that you like to be a student every chance you get. Why?

I believe that in order to be a good teacher you have to be open to new learning. I don't have any ego problems in becoming a student. Everybody feels awkward or clumsy the first time. You can get the best kickboxer in the world, and put him on the ground against a wrestler, and he's going to be like a kid – or vice versa. I realized that only when you put yourself in what I call an "insecurity position" can you really learn something. And when you learn something you get better. I don't mind being a student in savate, or Thai boxing, or wrestling. In fact I really like to be in that position. It probably has something to do with my personality. You need experiences to grow, and it's important for an instructor to remain a student in order to constantly seek better ways of training and teaching.

Do you think experience is the best teacher?

If not the best, then definitely one of the best. But having experiences without the understanding to evaluate and learn from them is not good. You have be able to understand your experiences – this is where knowledge takes place.

Is that why you like to give experiences to your students?

Right. If the student really wants to learn he will, despite the method or the system that the teacher is using. If the student doesn't want to learn, there's nothing the teacher can do. No matter how well the instructor can impart the knowledge, it's up to the student to have the desire to learn. This is the reason why every instructor has very good and very bad students. Some students only need to hear "Hands up!" one time, and they won't drop them again. For others, you have to correct that point class after class, for years and years, and they will still drop the hands!

You advocate change. What kind of change do you mean?

I think that a better word would be "adaptation" or "evolution." I don't think the term "change" is totally understood in martial arts because it gives the notion that you're changing styles all the time, when you're not. Let's say that I'm a boxer and I know nothing about kicking. If I have to face a kicker, some of the boxing aspects have to be slightly modified to deal with those kicks. The head can't lean forward, the block has to be adjusted to protect my face, et cetera. I'm not 'changing styles, but rather adapting my system.

If I face a fighter that likes to kick to the legs, like a Thai boxer or a savate man, I need to learn the technical knowledge for blocking those kicks. Otherwise, I'm going to get in trouble. So my defensive structure starts to be a little bit different because my weight distribution has to be different than the on-guard position that I was using in boxing – which would make my front leg very vulnerable. Of course, knowing how to kick will raise my offensive level and my attacking possibilities. I may still prefer my boxing hands to finish the fights, but I still need to adapt according to the opponent. We can introduce wrestling and groundwork into this, making the complete equation even more complex. But the whole idea is that the more you know, the better prepared you are.

I've always believed that learning was a process of accumulating knowledge. Sometimes the knowledge is not just a physical technique, but rather the understanding you get from the experience of training in other systems by learning their techniques and tactical approaches. As a fighter you can learn ten different ways of blocking a kick to your legs, and after many hours of sparring and trial-and-error, you might decide to use only two for your fights. The opponent may know your two techniques, and some people may think that this makes you predictable – but that's wrong. If you know how to use the tactics and the rhythm and timing with only two techniques, you can be very unpredictable in combat. But if you're an instructor you have to be very careful to never discard any knowledge because what may be useful for you (the two ways of blocking the low kicks) may not be useful for your students. So you have the responsibility to giving to the students the ten techniques for blocking the low kick and let them,

through experiences in sparring, decide which are the best for them. Knowledge is relative to the user and the practitioner. To understand certain experiences you need to have previously accumulated knowledge.

So trial and error is the key to learning?

For me it is. I introduced Bruce to the foam football shield and kicking shield around 1964. He rejected its usage because at that time he preferred to train solely on the heavy bag. I told him to experiment and work with it for a while, and after two weeks he fell in love with it. He even developed drills that he modified or changed as he got more familiar and learned more about it's usage. Let's take football. The difference between a rookie and a veteran is experience. A veteran is more knowledgeable than a rookie. His knowledge come from previously accumulated learning experiences. It is true that every moment is different, but one can better cope with a situation if he has the knowledge to flow from moment to moment. Only after you had many experiences can you "chisel away" the many nonessentials.

Do we have to accumulate knowledge then?

We have to be inspired by the previously accumulated knowledge and not to be bound by that previous knowledge – which is very different. That's why I encourage my students to study and look into other systems and instructors. No art, person or system is better than any other. It's important to understand not what is right in general, but what is right for the moment.

How important is it to know yourself, in your martial arts philosophy?

I think is paramount. Only you can answer certain questions – not your instructor, or your sifu – but only you. To understand yourself is the very beginning of the self-discovery process. If you lack of understanding about yourself, you become an ignorant, second-hand martial artist because you are the one in charge of expressing yourself and making the art work. And the only way you can do this is by being an expert on yourself.

You mentioned that teaching martial arts is a two-way street. Why?

Because good instructors produce good students and good students help the instructors to be better. Instructors should realize that everyone has his own path – that's why I would rather be a pointer to the truth than a giver of the truth. The teacher has to understand that the student will find his own way when he's ready. In fact, that's what the very essence of the JKD philosophy is all about.

What do you think about forms?

I have to say that Bruce was not anti-form and neither am I. Forms or katas are a way to learning proper body mechanics. Forms can be a part of your training, but your entire training shouldn't be based on them. They can be useful to structure certain knowledge so you can preserve it, but once you understand it you should freelance. You don't have to follow any particular sequence – you can flow. But as far as teaching is concerned, the instructor needs to have a format, a structure, and a technical progression in order to pass-on knowledge – even if later he discards that structure and mixes the material. The key is not to be bound by the form, but to learn from the form.

Some people might ask why Dan Inosanto is still seeking knowledge for other instructors if he personally trained with Bruce Lee? Wasn't Bruce Lee enough?

Bruce was a very knowledgeable and talented teacher –especially on one-on-one – but no one man has it all. Bruce himself went to study and research under different people because he realized that principle a long time ago. It is true that I do it more openly, perhaps due to my own personality. But make no mistake, Bruce wanted to liberate his students. He wanted no one to take his advice as gospel.

What are your personal goals as a martial artist and as a teacher?

I'd like to see my students develop themselves. They will take the arts in many different directions and that's fine as long as they don't insist that their way is the only way. A good martial arts instructor can be a combination of many things – from a guide and father figure, to a close friend and counselor. A truly good instructor may well be worth more that he could ever be paid, because there is not enough money to pay those who are so relevant to the development of your character, education, and confidence. My goal is to create a standard of excellence for all the martial art, regardless of origin, and to perpetuate the art and philosophy of Bruce Lee's Jeet Kune Do.

BEN LARGUSA

A SIMPLE MAN OF KALI

Ben Largusa, one of the highest ranking Filipino martial artists in the world, simply describes himself a man of kali — a system so effective in combat that some southern Philippine island tribes successfully resisted the armored steel might of the Spanish Empire for nearly four centuries. Kali is the source of all escrima styles and Largusa is widely regarded as the final word on this devastating and effective weapon. As the only student of Grandmaster Floro Villabrille, the Philippine's most revered fighter and victor of numerous stick-fighting "death matches," Largusa learned a unique blend of methods, strategies, and techniques unknown to any other man in the world.

As his years of training passed, Largusa realized that his training under Grandmaster Villabrille was primarily comprised of fighting techniques and theory. Because the only sparring experience he had was with Grandmaster Villabrille himself, Largusa realized that he could not teach the system the way it was taught to him. The genius of Ben Largusa soon became apparent when he broke down, step by step and move by move, Grandmaster Villabrille's complete system of kali. In recognition of this accomplishment, Floro Villabrille gave Ben Largusa a signed legal document designating him the sole heir to the Villabrille method.

On March 8, 1992 Grandmaster Floro Villabrille passed away, and Tuhan Ben T. Largusa automatically became the second grandmaster of the Villabrille-Largusa Kali System. Currently living in Kauai, Hawaii, Grandmaster Largusa continues to perpetuate the warrior art of kali and the Filipino culture as part of the legacy handed down to him by one of the most legendary fighters of modern times, Floro Villabrille.

ESCRIMA MASTERS

What was the legendary Floro Villabrille like?

First of all I would like to mention that Grandmaster Floro Villabrille was a man of great integrity. He had sound moral principles, and was very honest and sincere. He firmly believed that giving was more important than taking, and he proved that not only as a martial artist but also as a civilian by making numerous charitable contributions for athletic scholarships and equipment.

His first martial arts instructor was his uncle, Master Villagano, and after many years he decided to search for another instructor. Moving from island to island and village to village, he finally met the blind princess Josephina of the Pulahane tribe in Gandari, Samar. Honestly, it would take a book to describe this extraordinary man's traits, feats, and achievements. He came to Hawaii during his late teens and settled in Honolulu. He later married Trinidad Pontis and became a well-respected U.S. citizen because of his involvement in community affairs. He loved singing and dancing and was a natural performer on stage. He loved Frank Sinatra – whom he met while employed by MGM Studios in Hollywood. To maintain sharpness and harmony through the philosophy of "Individual Oneness" and "Universal Oneness," he would sometimes work out with karate, kung-fu, aikido, and judo men. Grandmaster Villabrille was also a proficient fisherman. Two of his specialties were throw-net and spear-fishing. Through kali training he developed powerful lungs that allowed him to stay underwater much longer than normal. The practice of kali and his self-development through the tulong pisage, or "triangle theory" enabled him to achieve high physical and metaphysical peaks. He contributed annual scholarships to a high school and provided the varsity football team with complete new uniforms. His advice was sought by political officials and candidates alike.

How did he decide to train under Princess Josephina?

Well, he didn't plan to do it – it just happened that way! After years of training under his uncle, Master Villagano, he decided to travel and find other teachers. As I said before, he went to the tribe of Pulahane, in Gandari. This tribe had the reputation of being very wild, and Grandmaster Villabrille was warned by many people to not make the trip. But he was sure nothing bad would happen to him because he had a positive reason to go there, wanted to learn, and also knew how to talk to people. He recited his oraciones or "prayers" so he could calm other people's anger by speaking nicely to them. He considered himself well-protected by the oraciones and by his pangkubal or "talisman."

So when he got there, and that was an adventure in itself, he approached the leader of the tribe and asked to meet the best kali teacher they had. The leader introduced him to a woman, blind from birth, named Josephina. After talking to her for a while, Grandmaster Villabrille told the leader that she was nice enough, but that he wanted to learn from their top master. The leader replied, "If you want to learn from the best, then you must study with her." Grandmaster Villabrille was surprised and could scarcely believe what the man was saying. Finally, with many misgivings, he agreed to try out the blind princess but to take it easy on her so as not to hurt her. Josephina approached and asked him to attack her any way he chose. The grandmaster was very skeptical and also afraid of hurting her, so he attacked very soft and slow. The princess easily blocked the attack and then told him to attack harder. This time grandmaster held back his power but not his speed, and was surprised how the princess could avoid the blows without being able to see. Finally, upon the princesses insistence, he started to hit fast and hard. Easily avoiding the blows, Josephina began to move in a way grandmaster never had seen before. What shocked him the most was that she was able to read the first blow with no previous contact or positioning information of any kind. He realized that the princess knew a method of fighting different from any he had seen before.

From his training under the blind princess, Grandmaster Villabrille developed a deep understanding of new principles and concepts such as offensive zoning, defensive zoning, minor and major movements, options and extensions, fluidity and sensitivity, large angle and small angle fighting, and the running attack. These principles made him look at kali from a very new and different perspective. A more sophisticated method of fighting was in front of him, independent of strength, power, and speed. The theories, principles, and laws of physics that he observed from Josephina allowed him to discover new and effective ways of training and fighting. He realized that everything Josephina did had an underlying principle and that understanding these concepts and principles was the key to his own personal development.

When did he decide to create his own method?

After training with Josephina, his kali no longer looked like the taught by his uncle, Master Villagano, so he decided to develop his own method. It's not that he invented or created a new style; he integrated the teachings of his uncle and the blind princess and formulated a cohesive structure and method once he went back to his home in Cebu.

What method did he use to train you in kali?

At the time I started training under Grandmaster Villabrille, the training was somewhat clandestine and I didn't have any sparring partners at all. For my training he used something he called the "four corners system," where I had to visualize imaginary opponents and react to different kind of attacks. Occasionally, he used to spar with me to check my progress in fluidity, angling, pivot points, de cadena, and my ability to react to an unexpected attack or counter. In his method of kali, we used different principles illustrated by geometrical designs like the "figure 8," "360-degree circle," and " Four leaf clover." Once you understand how these geometrical patterns work and how to look for them when you face your opponent, you'll be amazed by the number of techniques and possibilities you have. All of these pattern are incorporated in the logo used in the Villabrille-Largusa method, but it takes a qualified instructor to take you to the highest levels of application.

Were death matches truly to the death?

Let me clarify a misconception about death matches. I remember a top escrima instructor telling me that Felicisimo Dizon never competed in real death matches, because he lost one but was still alive.

Well, it is true that he did compete, did lose, and is still alive. Death matches did not always finish with one man dead. It was up to the winner to decide to kill the opponent or not. Of course, the defeated fighter would be maimed and crippled with broken bones and serious injuries – but if the winner decided to let him live it was well within his rights. Grandmaster Villabrille allowed many of his opponents to live, especially those who showed him respect before the fight. There were some other that were very cocky and disrespectful so Grandmaster Villabrille had no mercy with them. It all depended on the attitude of the opponent. He would mirror their intentions back to them. Unfortunately, and I need to really address this point here, a couple of books have been written in which Floro Villabrille was mentioned. One of these books stepped over the line of good journalism by saying he exaggerated some of his matches. He never had any reason to lie or exaggerate, nor did he ever have to ride on anyone's coattails to gain fame or notoriety. Many fighters did not walk over to their fallen opponent and deliver the death blow. Don't forget that the majority of the old escrimadors who fought in these death matches were honorable men, who, if they had the chance to spare the life of their opponent, did so. Not all of Grandmaster Villabrille's death matches ended in death.

In these death matches, how often was the rest of the body used such as fists, elbows, knees, and feet, for kicks and punches?

Very often! Stick fighting doesn't mean to fight only with the stick. The complete use of the body was necessary. The stick opened a lot of possibilities but in short range many times a kick, knee, elbow or punch was used with success.

How many death matches did Grandmaster Villabrille have during his lifetime?

Forty-four total – which it doesn't mean he only fought 44 times. That is the official record but he fought many other times that were never counted in his official record. He was never defeated. At that time, fighting and challenges were a common way of testing your skills. Through a challenge, you could find out whether a particular person was able to teaching you something or not.

What can you tell us about Grandmaster Villabrille's famous fight with the prince?

That's a very interesting story! Felicisimo Dizon was defeated by a tribal prince from Mindanao who was a Moro fighter. Dizon sent a telegram to Grandmaster Villabrille and told him about this fighter. Grandmaster Villabrille was 18 years old and was working on a ship at that time. The prince was really good and people said that he was like a kangaroo because his footwork was so good that when you tried to hit him in once place, he would bound to another almost before you struck. Grandmaster Villabrille decided to fight this man after learning of Dizon's defeat. Not wanted Floro to get hurt or perhaps even killed, his uncle Villagano tried to change his mind, but with no success. Grandmaster Villabrille isolated himself in the countryside and started his training for the fight. Training in nature allows you to interact with the forces of the Earth. The energy of the universe is there for you to grasp and your mind focuses with more power – with more energy. Being aware of this, Grandmaster Villabrille always trained in the open air, feeling the energy of the universe surrounding him. He realized that if his opponent was so fast with his footwork, he should be able of lure him in and then move back at the same time he delivered a powerful blow. This tactic of hitting while retreating allowing him to develop a very particular style of footwork. After practicing and perfecting this strategy, he became very proficient in moving back and delivering a finishing blow. Needless to say that during all this time he always recite his oraciones in order to receive the supernatural powers he needed to win. The oracion is a very important part of the art of kali and Grandmaster Villabrille always recited those even when he was not training for a fight.

What happened?

He came back and finally fought the Moro prince. In the beginning the prince was successful in moving in and out, but Grandmaster Villabrille had developed the strategy of allowing him to get close enough to hit – and that's what happened. The prince kept trying to strike, but the grandmaster moved out of range and returned powerful blows. Very soon, his uncle Villagano, who was in his corner, realized that Grandmaster Villabrille could handle himself and encouraged him to "fight his fight." Finally, grandmaster hit the prince with a blow to the neck that finished the match.

It's very interesting that Grandmaster Villabrille developed a certain type of footwork very similar to that used by Cassius Clay (Muhammad Ali) years later. Years later, Ali became the greatest boxer in history and you can see how he used to lure his opponents in and then counter them while he was moving back.

You mentioned that Grandmaster Villabrille never had a sparring partner and neither did you. How can you develop high fighting skills without any sparring?

This is not that simple to explain. In order to be a good fighter it is not necessary to be fighting all the time. The actual fight can be broken down into many components such as reflexes, sensitivity, coordination, footwork, power, body angling and positioning, et cetera. If you don't have any of these it doesn't matter how many times you spar – you'll never become a good fighter. This is because your foundation is weak. Through drills, we can develop all the necessary qualities for fighting. It's like football: the players drill and drills for the whole week – but they don't necessarily play actual games every day. What is very important is once you have all these qualities, you need to put the emotional aspect in there. When emotions are involved, then you're not drilling, you're fighting. Your attitude changes, like night to day. Your body is ready but you have to make sure that your mind also is.

Through the proper drills used in kali, you can get really close to actual sparring. For instance, if you understand the drill progression in sumbrada, you'll see that when you incorporate feints, enganos, half beats, et cetera and keep increasing the speed – it becomes a fight. Everything is unpredictable and hap-

ESCRIMA MASTERS

pens at high speed. You are actually drilling but it is close to a real fight. You can get seriously hurt if you're not careful. The higher the level of the drill, the closer to a real fight you are. The only difference is that when you have to fight, your mental and spiritual state is different.

When did you move to San Francisco?

When I was approximately 35 years old. Grandmaster Villabrille told me to train and spar with opponents of different styles. Once in the Bay Area I met some people from different karate and kung-fu styles. I remember being invited to a martial arts school and asked to spar with practitioners of choy lee fut, wing chun, and praying mantis. I could easily handle these fighters and the student asked the teacher how long did he thought I had trained in kung-fu. The teacher said a minimum of ten years each! It was very funny. The principles and art handed down to me by Grandmaster Villabrille allowed me to effectively deal with these other martial arts styles. At the time I was very strong and in incredible physical shape.

Kali, escrima and arnis are terms used generally to describe the Filipino martial arts; are they different names for the same art or different methods as well?

Kali is the ancient form of the martial arts of Indonesia and the Philippines. Before the Spanish colonization, the Philippines was always part of the old Indonesian empires back to the Sri Vishayan Empire in Sumatra in the 5th century with Hindu-Malayan influence by Arab missionaries. Chinese records note that in 983 AD a ship owned or commanded by an Arab and loaded with valuable merchandise arrived in Khanlu (Canton) from Ma-I or Mo-yi (the Mayid of the Arabs). Mai is an island in the Philippines. Eventually this led to Ma-I Nila on Maynila and then to Manila.

The old art of kali was always played alongside its counterparts, the other Indonesian martial arts of silat, pentjak, and kuntao. Kali was the martial art practiced by the Indonesians during the Indonesian empires. Tribal chieftains such as the sultans, datus, and rajahs and their warriors fought with this ancient art. Magellan and his men were defeated by Chief Lapu-Lapu and his warriors with kali – not escrima or arnis as is said and written in some places.

One theory says that the name came from "kalis," a bladed weapon; and the letter "s" was eventually dropped. Another theory says that "kali" came from the names "kaliradman," "kalirongan," and "pagkalikali." Still another theory says that the word comes from the first syllable of "kamut" (hand) and the first syllable of "Likok" (movements).

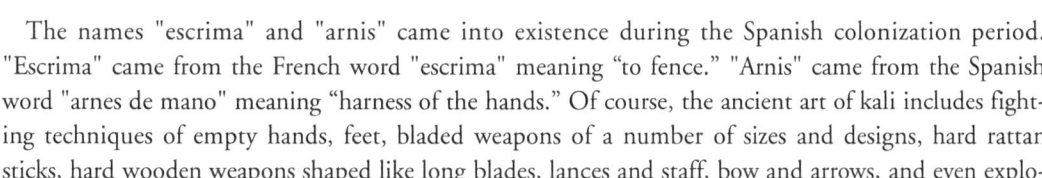

The names "escrima" and "arnis" came into existence during the Spanish colonization period. "Escrima" came from the French word "escrima" meaning "to fence." "Arnis" came from the Spanish word "arnes de mano" meaning "harness of the hands." Of course, the ancient art of kali includes fighting techniques of empty hands, feet, bladed weapons of a number of sizes and designs, hard rattan sticks, hard wooden weapons shaped like long blades, lances and staff, bow and arrows, and even explosive projectile weapons from guns to cannons. This makes an important difference. So "kali", "escrima," and "arnis" are not exactly the same.

How much influence did the Spanish culture really have on the Filipino martial arts?

Well, I believe we have to analyze this carefully. Culturally, the Spanish had a lot of influence. As far as the martial arts, and kali in particular, not that much. Please note that I'm talking about kali. In other methods such as arnis and escrima they did have more influence. Kali was already developed when they arrived, and if you look at the different methods of fighting and training you'll see that the Spaniard were mainly using what we call the small circle. Kali is based on the simultaneous use of the small and big circle. The Spaniards had big problems dealing with the kali men. The kali fighter used to move their weapons into the big circle, which completely surprised the opponent – since the Spanish had never seen an attack or defense from there – and placed them in a vulnerable position. This gave the kali fighter more than enough time to the small circle and finish the opponent.

Is the espada y daga method the basis of the Villabrille-Largusa system?

It is definitely a very important aspect of the art, and our system emphasizes this phase very much. The method of espada y daga opens many new possibilities to the student who has only trained in the single olisi (stick). It forces you to learn the use of the left hand in a more versatile way, for both defense and attack. In combat, the left hand become a very dangerous tool that can be used to finish your opponent. The very essence is that when facing an opponent with two weapons the empty, or alive, hand is in danger. It's very dangerous to block, monitor, or deflect an edged weapon with your empty hand. Using the espada y daga method, your left hand (where the dagger is in case you're right handed) can safely block the edged weapon without risk of being cut or damaged. Because of the training method, the left hand becomes more alive and reaches a new stage of combat skill. The possibility of seriously damage to the hand holding the dagger makes you aware of many other possibilities in combat. This aspect is definitely one of the most important in the Villabrille-Largusa method.

What about the sinawalli – the double stick phase?

This phase offers a more aggressive approach. Both weapons are long and the reach is bigger than if you use the espada y daga. Therefore, is more commonly used for attacking, since you have the reach advantage on your side. Part of the strategy is similar – but only part. Don't think that because you have two weapons they are meant to be used the same. The sophistication in the use of the dagger is different from the use of the double sticks.

Some Filipino instructors teach the art starting with the single stick, then proceed to espada y daga, sinawalli, dagger, et cetera. Do you teach phase by phase or you take the student through all the categories simultaneously?

In kali we try to make the student grow by themselves. If we teach only single stick and something

happens to the teacher, or the student has to move to another place, the practitioner will be limited and it will be impossible for him to evolve. However, if I teach the basics and fundamentals of every phase or category, the student will be able of develop even if I'm not with him. The idea is give the student enough tools to grow as a practitioner and not limit his evolution. Let's say that someone is able to training under me for the short period of time of two years. Well, after two years this student, instead of having only knowledge about the single stick, will have a fundamental understanding of the single stick, double stick, espada y daga, empty-hand methods, dagger, et cetera. He'll have the basis to keep growing and evolving. This is the main reason why I introduced this change in the teaching progression and methodology. I think is more beneficial for the student and the training is more enjoyable as well.

What can you tell us about the ranking system used in the Villabrille-Largusa system?

We have four different categories: the higher rank is called apohang tuhan and there is only one person in this level, which is currently myself. Then we have the tuhan. Only one person can have this title also. From level 7 to level 10 they are called "Professor," and from level 1 to level 6 they receive the title of "Guro." There is no limit to the number of professors and guros, but there is a limit for tuhan and apohang tuhan.

Would you please explain the Blood Ritual Ceremony?

In February of 1972, I gave the first public demonstration of the Villabrille system of kali in the Serramonte High School gymnasium, in Daly City, California. On that day I was presented with the red sash, elevating me to the rank of tuhan. This was made through the right of the Blood Ritual Ceremony, which was presided over and performed for the first time before the general public by Grandmaster Floro Villabrille. In this ritual, blood is drawn from the person to be promoted and from the person presiding over the ceremony. Each participant writes their name from the drawn blood on a piece of paper. The paper is then burned and the ashes are mixed with red wine in a chalice. After the proper prayers are recited, each participant then drinks from the chalice. It is from this ritual that the blood of Grandmaster Floro Villabrille continues to flow from generation to generation. All certified guros of the Villabrille-Largusa system go through this ritual.

You were a good friend of the late kenpo master Ed Parker – what can you tell us about him?

Ed Parker was a great man and a great martial artist with a very open mind. I remember he asked me about the art of kali and said, "Stickfighting, right?" I replied, "No, there is much more than just sticks." And I proceeded to show all the empty-hand movements and techniques. He was very surprised and decided we should get together more often. He loved the kali hand movements and footwork. We used to get together with another friend who was a choy lee fut practitioner. When Ed Parker decided to put his tournament together he asked me to demonstrate there. He knew that the more people there were around me the better I did! I guess I enjoyed the adrenaline rush of being on center stage! Those were great times.

Is it true that you were approached by Ed Parker to be Kato in The Green Hornet?

Yes, that's correct. Ed Parker had a lot of friends in Hollywood and was teaching some of the top people in the industry. To make a long story short, I got a call from Ed saying that Hollywood needed a person for that role and he thought of two people – myself and Bruce Lee – but he decided to offer the part to me first and Bruce second. I told him that I truly appreciated his offer but that I couldn't answer right then – that I needed time to think about it. I talked with my wife and after seven days I called Ed back and declined the offer. He was disappointed I didn't accept but he understood. "I'll have to call Bruce Lee," he said. And the rest is history.

Why you didn't accept?

I'm a family man. I had a wife and kids and I was really enjoying their company and seeing them grow up. I was never attracted to the world of Hollywood – that world has always seemed shaky to me. My wife actually told me, "Go! Do it if you want!" But I decided otherwise. The Hollywood world is not something I was dying to get into. I decided that my family was more important than fame. On the other hand, Bruce always wanted to be in Hollywood – it was his dream, he wanted it badly. He was ready to make any sacrifice to reach the top – and I wasn't. It was a matter of priorities, that was all. I met Bruce Lee several times after that – Bruce and I demonstrated together in Ed Parker's Internationals in 1964. But I never mentioned this to him and neither did Ed Parker. Bruce Lee deserves all the credit he has today – because he took his opportunity and made things happen for himself and others. He helped to popularize the martial arts like nobody else before or after.

ESCRIMA MASTERS

Did you ever regret not accepting Ed Parker's offer?

Not at all! I made a decision based on my personal principles; why I should regret anything? I had a great life, a good job I was truly enjoying, and a great family. Maybe I could have been a star, but maybe I would have lost something dear along the way. The things I could have lost were far more important to me that the glamour or stardom of Hollywood. It's true that sometimes you think, "What if had decided the other way?" But that is just human nature, right? Curiosity is human and that's all. No big deal.

I won't mention any names, but it is obvious that many masters and grandmasters of other styles learned from you, copied your movements, and adding those to their systems without giving you credit. How do you feel about that?

Well, let me put it this way, I could say they are copycats, but I would rather look at them as people who were touched by what I had to offer – they took kali into their lives and it improved whatever they were doing. As far as giving no credit to me – I don't really care. I know who I am, and what my art is all about. That's all I can say.

What to you feel about the idea of mixing different martial arts styles?

You have to be careful with mixing styles. Sometimes it can be beneficial and sometimes not. It's important to have an strong base and foundation. Once you have this, it is not that necessary to incorporate many other things. You may look for some specific elements that help you to improve what you have, but you don't necessarily have to add more and more just for the sake of adding. If a martial art system is used for fighting then there's not too much to be added – if you do anything I think "integrating" would be a better term. As I said I don't really believe in studying many different styles of martial arts and putting them together to create a new system. Sometimes martial artists do this because they don't think what they have is truly useful. It's important to notice that a technique may look not effective at first sight, but after further analyses you may find out that a slight adjustment in the angle will make the difference. Sometimes a couple of inches in the body angle will give you a different view of what you're doing. What is important is to find a system that allows you to be efficient and competitive in the different ranges and situations. Then it is more a matter of polishing and refining what you have rather than adding movements to the style.

Did you modify what Grandmaster Villabrille taught you?

Not in the technical sense. I realized that in order to properly teach the art you needed a progression, a way of organizing the material so the students could go from A to Z and grow at the same time and at the proper pace. The way I was taught by Grandmaster Villabrille was a very intuitive one. I never had any sparring partners and all my training was one-on-one. When I started to teach I found out I couldn't apply the same method. Therefore, I decided to structure what I was taught by my teacher. It's not that I changed or altered the techniques, but I did organize them in a more cohesive and comprehensive way. I did this so the students in the class could follow a logical progression in their training, going from one step to another in an organized way. I understand that some people may think that some "original flavor" has been lost through this process. But I truly believe that nothing has been lost and a lot has been gained since this allowed me to reach many more people who were interested in learning the art of kali.

How important are the spiritual aspects of kali?

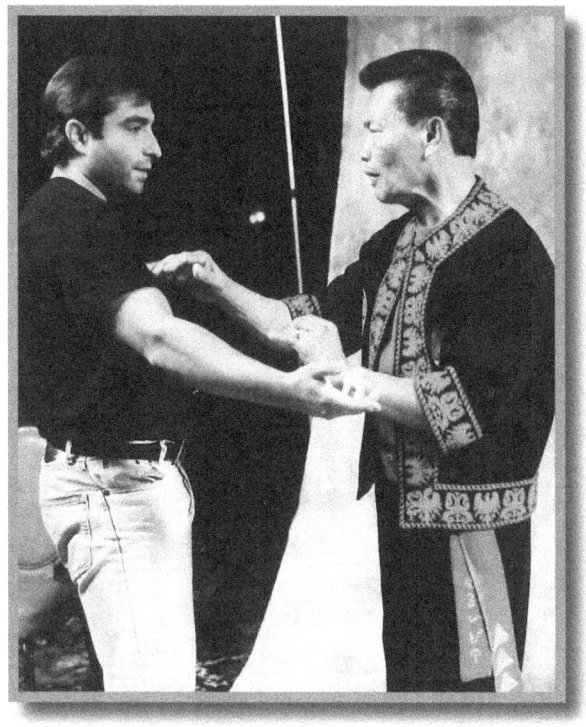

Very important. Grandmaster Villabrille mentioned that the oracion is as important as the physical techniques. Don't forget that a fighting art without philosophy and spirituality is only brutality. Without the spiritual and mental aspects one moves mechanically, like a robot, with no feeling or meaning. The oracion is important because it makes our minds stronger and develops our fighting spirit, what we can call plain old guts or courage. Everybody has a different degree of courage, and you either born with or without it. Now with kali spiritual training one doesn¹t have to be born with courage – it can be developed. In the same way that our emblem, with the internal, external and rhythm triangles and circle, represents all the possible actions and teaches how to break down the angles, attacks and counter-attacks when facing an opponent. The oracion allows us to reach the higher levels of spirituality and mental conditioning for training, fighting, and even daily life.

What did kali bring into your life spiritually?

A lot of things, but mainly peace, love, wholesomeness, and a oneness with others who love the art. Who could ask for anything more?

RENE LATOSA

A HIGHER LEVEL OF MARTIAL ART

Rene Latosa has been studying and teaching the Filipino martial arts for more than three decades. He began his training in 1968 and has studied under such masters as Dentoy Revillar, Serrada style, Max Sarmiento, Cadena de Mano style, Leo Giron, Larga Mano style, and Angel Cabales, Serrada style. However the most influential man in his life was his father, Juan Latosa. The training under his father's tutelage was far from easy and comfortable. The elder Latosa forged his son in the harshest and most difficult elements of the traditional Filipino arts and shaped in Rene's mind, the basic structure that would one day become the Latosa Escrima system.

In 1973, Rene Latosa left Stockon, California for duty in the U.S. Air Force and taught the SWAT teams of the local law enforcement agencies. This was the first time that local police had used the Filipino arts in their training. It was an exceptional opportunity for Master Latosa to test some of the theories used in developing his system.

Now retired from the Federal Government, Master Rene Latosa is known for never hiding information from his students, but freely sharing his knowledge and experiences to make the Latosa Escrima one of the most effective methods of Filipino martial arts in the world.

How long have you been practicing martial arts?

I started at the age of 17, and I have been practicing for about 33 years. It has been a 33-year learning experience. I am confident that I will continue to learn and discover more during the next 33 years. I initially started in the Serrada system under Grand Master Angel Cabales in Stockton, California. At that time the school had many visitors and people who just liked to train. I also trained with Maximo Sarmiento who was proficient in a Cinco Teros system, and was the best Cadena de Mano (empty hand) and knives expert that I have ever seen. Then there was Dentoy Revilar who was Angel's protégé, and

extremely talented. Another well-known master at the school was Grand Master Leo Giron, who taught us Largo Mano and other combat techniques. Being one of three students at the school, I was surrounded by a flood of Filipino martial arts information, and I reveled in the one-on-one attention. There was a variety of old men at the Filipino Center where I also practiced, who would pass by and offer up a secret technique to counter someone else's secret technique. My Father was my last instructor of any great length. His system didn't really have a name. In the Philippines he had trained in several different systems and at secret camps in the mountains.

What were the teaching methods like?

Angel Cabales would train us one on one. He believed in this method of teaching. There weren't very many students so it worked to our advantage. As the school grew, many students were being ignored or forgotten so Angel had to adjust to group training. There was nothing formal or anything that resembled rank. Angel was the master, then came Max, then Dentoy – that was the pecking order. Again, your training depended on who the instructors wanted to work with during the time they wanted to teach. Much of the time was taken up with countless hours of stories about their many experiences. I would sometimes be at the school until 11.30 at night talking and training with Max. He had great stories about his early days in San Francisco's Chinatown.

The training I obtained from my father was very intense. His only method of teaching was for me to strike at him and observe how he executed his movements as he struck back. There was no time for any trial and error. I knew he cut me some slack, though, because my Uncle Pedro got the same lessons when he was younger and he ended up always getting hit. My father would emphasize that attitude in a fight is just as important as movement. He said you must be brave or you will lose. In other word, he rarely moved back; he used forward pressure and constantly knew where his power was based.

What was your childhood like?

My father was a very influential individual in the Stockton Filipino community. He often watched me perform demonstrations with Angel at various grand openings and functions, and I would always be introduced as "Johnny's son." I did so many demonstrations that I began to feel very invincible – I was fast, strong, and my timing was on. My ego really got the best of me at the age of 18. One day while practicing at home, I needed someone to feed me some hits; my father was gardening so I asked him literally if he would be "my dummy." He just looked at me and continued gardening. When I asked him again, he dropped his shovel and walked over to me. I used to be very afraid of my father because he had a big voice, was very strong, and yelled at everyone – but now that I was a skilled warrior my fear vanished. He picked up a stick and said, "Hit me." I just looked at him as if he was playing with fire. I explained with a bit of an attitude, that I needed to practice and didn't have time to fool around. He asked me again to hit him, so I gave him a real easy, soft hit so as not to hurt the old man – and I felt a stick land hard enough on my head to get my attention. I explained the dangers of using a weapon you can't control, and he ask me to hit him again, and this time I hit him slightly harder and faster, and it ended up with the same result, a stick on my head. I was getting angry because twice this accident happened. He wanted another hit and I thought I would fake him out and tap his head, and then block his strike. So I faked the hit and again his stick landed on my head and this time he was laughing. I went for him and he moved his stick hit me on the shoulder and I fell to the ground. He put the stick down and went back to gardening. My mother was watching and told him to stop tormenting me. As I brushed myself off, feeling bewildered, frustrated, and ready to give up, my father explained to me that he was the top fighter in his region – not a sports fighter but a real fighter. From then on I listened and learned all I could. The funny thing was that everyone in the older community knew how good he was but no one ever told me. Even when I visited his village in the Philippines, there was a look of confusion as well as amusement when I asked the old men at the square about finding a master I could train with. They kept telling me, "Go home and see your papa."

How has your escrima developed over the years?

Sometimes your natural talent comes into play. If I wasn't a natural at escrima, I had to become one fast. My father taught one way – which was to hit me. When I tried to get him to show me a movement again, he would demonstrate five different moves – none of which looked like the one I asked about. He said he didn't know how to do a single technique for a single attack. He reacted on instinct and his movements were based on the intent of the opponent coupled with his own fears. Early on I realized I could mimic any system I saw, by looking at it conceptually and not technically. Escrima has not changed, but rather my method of teaching has. For example, pro-football coaches saw the need to enhance individual skills and in order to do this they developed certain drills to develop these attributes. A defensive lineman's job is to protect the quarterback. It takes more skills than just being big and strong. The skilled athlete needs awareness of the field, the proper use of their body weight, watching the body language of the opponent, and a quick explosion off of your stance. The elements utilized by the skilled athlete are timing, explosiveness, balance, and proper center of gravity. Each of these elements is necessary to the development of a lineman, and each of these elements is practiced separately and then put together to achieve peak performance. To me, the martial arts are exactly the same; you need to develop each skill, and transition this into the execution of the technique. In my teaching I have five basic concepts which I use in every technique. These concepts consist of power, focus, speed (timing and distance), balance, and transition.

Much of my teachings focus on the individual concepts. For example, when I teach power I want the students to achieve the maximum amount of power their body can generate. Then the students will know and understand what is achievable. Once they understand maximum power, the trick is to understand how to balance power and use it to your advantage. Sometimes generating that much power doesn't leave you much room to recover if you miss your target. A boxer throwing a hook at full power every time, usually falls off-balance, and eventually the other boxer will read this and take advantage of

ESCRIMA MASTERS

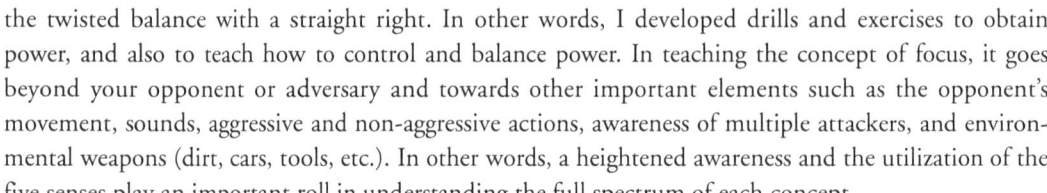

the twisted balance with a straight right. In other words, I developed drills and exercises to obtain power, and also to teach how to control and balance power. In teaching the concept of focus, it goes beyond your opponent or adversary and towards other important elements such as the opponent's movement, sounds, aggressive and non-aggressive actions, awareness of multiple attackers, and environmental weapons (dirt, cars, tools, etc.). In other words, a heightened awareness and the utilization of the five senses play an important roll in understanding the full spectrum of each concept.

Do you think there is still a "pure" system as taught by masters such as Angel Cabales, Leo Giron, and Ben Largusa – or we are going to a more "mixed" approach?

I really don't think there ever was a pure style. Everyone has their own version or interpretation of what they know and what was taught to them. I am not so sure a pure system can exist because of all the influences and experiences one draws on when teaching. I am certain that every individual injects his own meaning, individual innovations, and creativity – which obviously influences any system. I think different styles help people to understand what elements tie these arts into the Filipino martial arts. Personally, I feel a person can study any system they want; the effectiveness depends on that person's ability to execute the right concepts to make it work. No style is effective unless you can hit your target. In order to hit your target, you need to understand the concept of distance, how much speed is necessary, and the coordination of these two efforts, which gives a person their timing. I actually had a person come up to me and tell me that they are one of the fastest stick practitioners in the world. So I grabbed his throat and said, "So what's your point?" Speed doesn't help you unless you know how to use it, which also means understanding the concept of balance.

Tournaments help to develop some of these qualities and have their place in the martial arts. I set up my tournaments to have value, not to find out who the best fighter is in the world. My concept of a tournament is training. Tournaments are drills to find the relationship between distance, timing, and speed. In a full-contact escrima tournament, there is an obvious safety factor, so in this instance you will not learn about power, since power becomes a moot point with safety equipment and the safety of others. In a fight, the fastest guy in the world is not the most dangerous if he doesn't hit his target. I want tournaments to help students realize that the timing of a hit depends on how fast you can close the distance or work the distance when you see the opening. The second most important aspect of tournaments is assuring that the students maintain balance. Balance is one of my main concepts – everything else revolves around it. Tournaments should be used to learn specific parts of the martial arts. Obviously, it is also fun because of the adrenaline rush and the competitive spirit. In our tournaments punches and kicks are allowed.

Do you think no-holds-barred events bring positive or negative aspects to the martial arts?

I don't think it is mainstream enough to bring any negative aspect to the martial arts. I personally love a good fight – or rather like to see a good fight. Besides, unless it is on TV, like the Friday night fights, I don't think the general public will find it very interesting. The new movies on the other hand like Crouching Tiger, Hidden Dragon and Rush Hour 2 are mainstream and seem to overshadow these type of extreme fighting events.

Do you think that martial arts in the West has caught up to the level of the Philipines?

I think so. In today's shrinking world, everyone has the opportunity to look at what athletes are doing in their training and the physical size of today's individuals. Take football for example; 10 to 15 years ago, being 6 foot tall and weighing 200 pound would have been big enough to play a lineman. A person today of that size may not even make the team. The training level an athlete can achieve is very progressive, and the martial arts have to progress in the same manner. Look at boxers in the 1970's who were considered heavyweights, and then look at the size of today's heavyweights. They are two different weight classes now.

Are martial arts a sport or a way of life?

Certain areas of the martial arts can be called a sport, but the martial arts are very complex because of the emphasis on tradition, self-defense, and reality usage. The competitive spirit in sports is the opposite of the martial arts. We were taught to be humble and not use the art in a way that shows arrogance. In a combat sport you have to have this or you will never get to the next level.

Do you think it helps students to physically to train with weapons?

I think it is important for the student to experience the weapons essence. In other words, its weight, length, density, how balanced or out of balance it feels, and understanding when and where the weapon is the most powerful. For example, with a chain, at what point does it achieve the most power or impact? On the other hand, if you wrap the chain around your hand, the power structure of the weapon changes. So training with weapons also means understanding the attributes of the weapon. There is 100 percent teaching in empty-hand and weaponry phases. Because I use concepts to teach, when you learn weaponry you can automatically transfer what you learned to your empty hands. Logically, if the weapon is an extension of the hand, then there should be no difference other then adjusting for the length of the weapon and the distance between you and your opponent. An instructor must understand the real meaning of transition from weapons to empty hands.

Do you have any general advice to pass on?

Be truthful, logical, and question what you are taught. Make sure that everything you are taught has a purpose, a meaning, can be used, and is flexible in any situation. Secondly, practice from a natural standing position. Most people practice in a somewhat safe environment such as a school, which means practicing with a person in front of you who you know is going to attack. The point is you are practicing being reactive instead of being proactive. Why did you wait and let the person get close enough to attack? Did you not notice the aggressive behavior? As the person got close did your hands get into a

ESCRIMA MASTERS

position that didn't display aggressiveness yet protected yourself? Did you prepare for an attack or wait until the attack was coming? If you waited to see whether you were going to be attacked, then you have to depend on your speed and hope you are faster then your attacker. What is overlooked at times, during practices, is the fact that the person attacking may be as fast as you and as skilled. That being the case – and all things being equal – then the attacker has the edge. On the other hand, a practitioner's personal training is closely associated with how they teach their students. As an instructor, you can see your influence on the students. If the student does not understand the point you are trying to make, you, as the instructor, must try to find a different route to comprehension. Each time you do this, you learn to think outside the box.

What are the major changes in the arts since you began training?

The two major changes are the open teaching method and reality training. I break down every aspect of a movement, especially those unique to the Filipino martial arts, and substantiate the reason for its use. There are movements in the Filipino martial arts that people train in and are led to believe that work. I want my students to feel free to challenge what they are practicing when they feel uncomfortable. I want the students to believe in what they practice. I want students to think for themselves rather than taking my word that the movement works. On the reality side, I feel students must practice as if there is no second chance and must make what they know work the first time. From the stick twirling, locks, stabs, fakes, and to all the movements associated with the figure-eight's, the students must validate these movements within themselves. I train to become more efficient and to eliminate wasted movements while assuring the concepts I teach are still in place. I also teach with the attitude that a person must be able to read their opponent, or in other words, hit your opponent before he hits you. This training teaches to not only read an attack, but also to have the ability to instantly change a defensive posture to an offensive one.

Who would you like to have trained with that you have not (dead or alive) and why?

One person would be Japanese swordsman Musashi – because he was straightforward, he anticipated the results and the opponent, and simplicity was his expertise. The second would be my Great Grandfather Esteban. The main reason would be to see the Filipino martial arts back in his day. I would like to see his skill level, the effectiveness of his skills, and the types of opponents he was confronted with.

What keeps you motivated to train after all these years?

The look on my students' faces when they make an application work. The pleasure I get when they thank me for teaching them the knowledge I have given them. Lastly, I take pride in continually sharing my Filipino culture and heritage through the martial arts. Of course, there is always further to go in any form of study. The quest for knowledge never ends. When something is at the pinnacle of perfection, it can always be improved on. Study means learning, and every time you teach you learn something new – whether it is from what you may discover or what you may have seen your students do. No one is immune from learning more, discovering more, and creating more.

The marital arts is an equalizer. If you get into a situation, the martial arts gives you the ability to equalize physical size, strength, natural ability, and experience against a normal opponent. For example, if someone bigger wants to start trouble, you know you can get the advantage by kicking him in the groin. Thus you equalized his size by using skill and knowledge. Now if the attacker is highly skilled in the martial arts and is bigger and stronger, the outcome will depend on who is better skilled, who gets to hit first in the right spot, who impedes who's balance first, and who maintains control of the offense. So my point is, I will always be honest with my students and have them keep the martial arts in the right prospective. As in any endeavor anyone undertakes, a person must pay his dues with hard work and practice while understanding the basic concepts of the martial arts.

Is it necessary to engage in free-fighting to achieve good street-fighting skills?

Free-fighting certainly raises the level of understanding the distance, timing and speed necessary to find an opening and respond to the opening. Much like any sport, certain training gets you in tune for the opportunity. In football, as a running back, you must see an opening between two defensive linemen and shoot for the hole. If you hesitate, someone is coming at you because you are an easy target. Free fighting gives you a sense of reality without the full danger of combat. It allows you to make mistakes and live to fight another day. Fighting on the streets is without any sort of gentlemen's rules – anything goes. So if you are free-fighting, at least your skills are somewhat practiced and your percentage of survival moves up a couple of percent. Don't forget, luck and awareness is a huge factor in wining a street fight.

What's your opinion about mixing different Filipino styles?

If you look at it like an educational institution, a student with a well-rounded education mixes math with economics, history, language and perhaps with a spot of tennis. In this society, knowledge is a key element in developing a person. Knowledge in the martial arts does not mean memorizing a technique, but learning why the technique works. Mixing martial arts' styles is just getting to the same point by choosing a different road. When a person reaches the pinnacle of a specific martial art, they should have reached the pinnacle of all martial arts. I would like to think that what I teach is usable and effective – that what I teach is the truth. In other words, when someone leaves my seminars I know that I didn't fill up the seminar time with useless movements or busy drills but useful information. Secondly, I like to raise the normal rate of retention for the students. I always want people to obtain good value when they come to seminars and to remember what was taught. It would be like going to a movie and forgetting the plot because there was so much action to distract you.

ESCRIMA MASTERS

Do you have a particularly memorable training experience?

When I opened my school in San Francisco, I decide to train my students to not concern themselves with anything but reaction and movement – to attack and win at all costs. I taught them a simple five-strike box system. Two weeks later a group of students from another school came by and wanted to work out and I said OK. I had one side throw a strike and then the other side do the same – that way we could train regardless of system or style. The outside group was the first to throw to my new group of students who had no training in formalities or anything else other then pure fighting. The outside group kept asking my students what they wanted for a strike and my group didn't care because we never practiced that way. When it was my student's turn to throw strikes, the outsiders kept tapping their sides, and their shoulders indicating where they wanted the hits to land. Since my students had no idea what they wanted they hit them anywhere they pleased and threw them all off-balance again and again. They soon left, although a few came back to ask how long my students were training because they thought they were pretty good and would it be possible for them to train with us. I told them my students had just started two to three weeks earlier – the look on these higher-level student's faces, which was priceless.

How do you think a practitioner can increase their understanding of the spiritual aspects of the arts?

I believe we are all spiritual beings. Our personal understanding or beliefs and our journey along that path is very individual. Discipline and practice in any art form is meditation. For example, the runners high experienced by a dedicated runner, and the loss of time an artist experiences as they paint a canvas are all forms of meditation and a glimpse into our spiritual essence. As you exercise, practice, and acquire discipline in the martial arts you will become aware and in touch with your inner or spiritual self.

Martial arts is like so many other endeavors we begin in our lives. There is the initial thrill of learning new things, being a part of something, and practicing until you get it right. I figure that after about two years, a person starts to contemplate whether they are making the right investment of money, time, and effort. At this point, you may look around and see other people who may have natural talent and can learn easier, and your confidence level goes down. This is the point where people make a decision to continue training or find a new thrill. Obviously, there are certainly more reasons than this, but this is just one scenario.

What do you consider to be the most important qualities of a successful martial artist?

There are several ways of defining a successful martial artist. Are you successful because you have hundreds of students, because you turned out some very good martial artists, because you have been credited with giving inspiration, or because you are the fastest, strongest or most talented? I think the most important quality of a successful martial artist is being a thoughtful human being. Everyone should be treated fairly, and with respect and dignity. Just because you are titled as a master, grandmaster or whatever does not change your status as a human being. These titles are only reflective of your skill and knowledge. If you have worked very hard and earned a title, then by all means you deserve it; but it is an honor that should not be abused. More knowledge is good, as long as it is the truth or it is something you enjoy. Sometimes I feel that people take the martial arts too seriously and collect too many titles, too many ranks, and not enough enjoyment. We must never forget the thrill of learning something new, discovering why things work, and making movements that don't work, work.

Have ever felt fear in your training?

My fear is the fear of accidentally hitting someone I am training with, because they thought it might be fun to get in a hit when they saw an opening. There are always those students who come at you like gangbusters because they feel you won't hurt them. The essence of training is taking in knowledge – not trying to win. I hit outrageously hard and I know the damage I can inflict. Because I have trained all my life in being aware of everything, I react to sudden and unwarranted movements. When you are trained to react, my response is usually automatic – and I could easily end up hurting someone very seriously. Students sometimes forget I am there as a teacher, not trying to be the

biggest baldest dude in the world – but they still must remember I have always been trained to instinctively protect myself at all times.

It is important to always see the truth in what you do. I know everyone says this, but they have to look deep into what they do and ask themselves whether what they do works. If there is any doubt, and you are only doing it because that is the way you were told, then you must explain to your students that it is being done to preserve the art and keep it intact. For an instructor to let a student out on the streets, knowing that it only works in a school environment, is like sending someone out to battle a bear using a butter knife.

What are your thoughts on the future of the martial arts?

The martial arts should be geared toward the next generation. Students should focus on the style and quality of instruction they are receiving, and the role models they will have to follow. Martial arts politics always hurt the students because they suffer for the wants and needs of a few. The reason we got involved and the reason we teach the martial arts seems to diminish as people start looking around and concerning themselves with what other people think, who said what about who, who is better then anyone else, and who will steal who's students. The idea of the martial arts is a way of living life. You set a goal and you accomplish it and work on making it more efficient. If you can accomplish a high level in the martial arts, then perhaps nothing is out of reach and your potential is limitless. As a teacher, your students look to you as a role model and will act similar towards the next generation. Martial artists should also understand that instructors, masters, and gurus are just people like themselves. The fact that they may have more knowledge does not make them better than anyone else.

SEAN LONTAYAO

A FAMILY JOURNEY

AFTER MANY YEARS OF TRAINING AND DEDICATION TO THE ART OF KALI UNDER THE GUIDE OF HIS FATHER GM GREG LONTAYAO, SEAN LONTAYAO KEEPS WALKING THE SAME PATH, IMMERSING HIMSELF IN THE PRACTICE OF HIS BELOVED ART. ACCORDING TO LONTAYAO, NATIONALITY SHOULD NOT MATTER. IF YOU CAN UNDERSTAND THAT EVERYONE IS CREATED EQUAL, WHAT DIFFERENCE DOES OUTSIDE APPEARANCE MAKE IF THE SPIRIT, MIND, AND BODY ARE TRULY IN LOVE FOR THE ART OF KALI.

WITH ONE FOOT PLANTED IN THE PAST AND THE OTHER ROOTED IN THE PRESENT, LONTAYAO IS CONSIDERED BY MANY TO BE ONE OF THE BEST KALI INSTRUCTORS IN THE WORLD, BUT HIS GOAL HAS NEVER BEEN TO GLORIFY HIMSELF, BUT RATHER TO PRESERVE ALL THE KNOWLEDGE PASSED ONTO HIM BY HIS TEACHER IN ORDER TO PERPETUATE THE ART.

"COMING FROM A PURE ART BACKGROUND," SAYS LONTAYAO, "I CAN APPRECIATE THE UNIQUENESS OF BEING DIFFERENT. THE FUTURE SHOULD BE AN EXTRAORDINARY ADVENTURE THAT CAN SIGNAL RARE AND FANTASTIC VISIONS OF THE ACCUMULATED KNOWLEDGE SITTING AT OUR DOORSTEP. THOSE LEADERS AMONG US SHOULD BE ABLE TO LOCATE AND LEARN FROM SUCH CONTRIBUTING INDIVIDUALS, TEACHERS AND MASTERS. THE ONGOING EFFORT TO PROBE OUR PERSONAL INTELLECT, PHYSICAL ABILITIES, AND SPIRITUAL POWERS SHOULD NOT CEASE IN OUR LIFETIME BECAUSE OF INTERNAL OR EXTERNAL LIMITS."

How long have you been practicing Filipino Martial Arts, and who were your teachers?

I started Kali in 1972 at the age of six. My teachers were not only Filipino Martial Artists but Martial Artists in general. I started with my Father Professor Greg Lontayao and my brothers Greg, Jimmy, Jay and my sisters Gina and Mykie. My mother, Loretta Sojot Lontayao, supported us all and had a big part in establishing a family's history filled with Martial Arts memories.

ESCRIMA MASTERS

I acknowledge my Godfather, Grandmaster Ben Largusa and my Grandfather and Uncle, Graciano Lontayao Sr. and Professor Clarence Lontayao, as teachers. I would also acknowledge all eighty one of my father's Black Belts along with all the students of the Lontayao Martial Arts Organization because to teach is to learn /to learn is to teach.

There are three Grandmasters who have supported my father and have been there in my life that I may have not learned directly from but have watched me as I progressed in the Martial Arts. They are Grandmaster Fred Lara Internal poison hand system, Grandmaster Ming Lum Choy Li Fat and Grandmaster Floro Villabrille of the Villabrille/Largusa Kali system.

How many styles of Martial Arts have you trained in?

I have trained in the Shiki Shin Funi, Kenpo and Kaji Kumi Karate, and Kali. Parts of our training also included Judo and even boxing and wrestling techniques. Shiki Shin Funi which in the name describes an art that's not style, but a way. The physical aspects include Okinawan, Japanese, Korean and Chinese influence the deeper the study gets. These consist of basic arm exercises called the A-10, basic stands called the Dachi and the basic eight kicks called the Geri. Kenpo Karate and Kaji Kumi Karate had fist styles and striking styles that can be related to Kung Fu styles White Crane, Praying Mantis and Hung gar.

My father ran a school for nine years in South San Francisco, CA behind Brentwood Bowling Alley off of El Camino Real. This school was also the location of the first commercial school of Kali under the Largusa School of Kali. Training was strict; discipline was key. We trained for two hours straight with no breaks in between. We trained barefoot on hard concrete floors covered in tile that had cracks. There was no air-conditioning, mats or mirrors, and once you were in line you didn't move or touch your Gi or your belt and you stood and listened to lectures. You didn't talk during class or look around, you stood at attention. With all of this at a young age, you learned what Martial Arts are. The Dojo was filled with adults and kids of all ages and I was the youngest.

We practiced Judo in which we learned grabs, how to push and pull, sweeps, throws and tumbles and learning how to fall. When we did Judo throws we used tatami mats. We had lessons in Boxing and used boxing gloves, headgear, a big heavy leather medicine ball, and an old white EverLast punching bag that was rock solid on the bottom. We also had two makiwara boards, jump ropes for exercising and developing rhythm and timing and building leg strength and to build endurance. Drills in jabs, right hooks, left hooks, upper cuts and combinations and of course getting hit in the face when sparring. I also had the opportunity to be the practice guy for my neighbor and another friend of mine, who used to challenge each other to see how fast they could pin me. They had some serious wresting skills and were State Champs their senior year in High School.

In Kali you begin with bladed weapons or sticks in your hands and you learn it's an extension of the arm. When using the weapon you use the big circle so you use the full length of the weapon, not necessarily outside fighting because you want to be able to use the shorter weapon (daga) to enter the thrust when your opponent comes too close and or check your opponent. This makes up for one style called "Numerado" which is inside fighting and in order to stay inside, you ride the blow. All of Kali's theories are governed by the 360-degree circle which leads to one strike into another or redirecting a strike defensively or offensively and gaining momentum and applying opposite directional force and redirecting your opponent. The agaw (disarming) is practiced with either a blade or dagger being attacked at all angles and the grabs, pulling and steps are similar to Aikido. From the day I started there was one exercise all styles had in common and it was the breathing exercise. In 1992 only then did I get to begin the training in cultivating chi and begin the transition from internal to external to all physical aspects.

Would you tell us some interesting stories of your early days in Kali?

Early days for me was when you see rattan sticks being cut with a hand saw in the back yard then being soaked under water in the bath tub weighed down by weights to be straightened. Then later stained and hung up to dry. Then later 1" tape on each end, so that when your holding your stick you have a 1" gap and when you strike your opponent only the tip where the tape is that's the part of the stick used or little more as long as you use the full length of your weapon, that's the idea.

These were sticks that were used in some of the first group demonstrations bringing Kali out to the public in San Francisco Civic Center where the CKC Karate tournaments took place in the early 70's by the Ralph Castro family. I could remember when the whole place was dark except for the floor in the middle being lit up by spot lights. At a young age, the Civic Center seemed huge with high ceilings… the place was just big. We had on our beige vest and pants with trimming and moccasins that you could slide in. We would run out twirling our sticks heading towards the center under the lights and start demonstrating. The Center was pitch black except for the spot light on only us demonstrating Kali and the whole place was silent. I remember early mornings me and my father would go to my Godfathers Grandmaster Largusa's house in Pacifica, CA. I would sit in the living room with Romper Room on and something to eat and drink, while they talked for hours in the kitchen. I was too young to know what they were talking about. When I reached my mid twenties I asked my father what they were talking about and he told me that he helped the Grandmaster create the ranking system and write the by-laws for the Villabrille Largusa System of Kali. They had to set the by-laws and the standards if they wanted to teach and spread Kali out to the public. There were a few changes many years later.

Were you "natural" at Kali - did the movements come easily to you?

No, I was not natural at all. I learned just like everyone else. I remember as if it was yesterday. On one early evening everyone was ready to go to Karate class. As my mother was getting me "dressed" standing in between her and my father I heard the word Karate. I looked at my mom and asked, "Can I join Karate?" She looked at my Dad then looked at me and said go find a Gi. I ran up the stairs opened the closet and dug into the pile looking for my size. The difference between me and my brothers and sisters is I asked to join and they had no choice. Kali just fell into place, I was there and Kali was there.

One night you're handed a stick and you're holding it, it becomes fascinating holding a stick and being introduced to this weapon and you're taught right away to keep all five fingers around your weapon always. That lesson is always given and never forgotten. At the age I started, the moves didn't have to be perfect and as long as I wasn't playing around I was okay. Everybody probably remembers what I used to do in class more than me. I think it helped learning with everyone being older because the attention is on them and you watch when they get corrected you correct yourself before they come around to you. You watched, you listened, and just followed. I remember when Lindsey, my God-brother, would come around and fix the positioning of the sticks. My God-brothers, my God-sister, my brothers and sisters and cousins were in their teens and they were all good, "seriously good". This is what was "natural" and "traditional" was that it started with the families.

How has your personal expression of Kali has developed over the years?

Kali is what I learned it to be. I feel there is nothing missing in my relationship with Kali. I feel free with Kali. I keep Kali under the light and the light is bright. Always have good intentions, stay on the right path, be truthful and be respectful. When it's placed around you, you can't grow out of it just grow with it. As I get older it just gets more interesting scratching the surface and uncovering more to learn. I don't ask nor do I seek for any "recognition" or "acknowledgement" and most of all "rank". What was given to me is for me to give back.

Do you think different "styles" are truly important in the art of Kali?

Yes, different styles are important. A little of everything is good. They are important to observe, and learn if given the opportunity. It's you the fighter who uses what works, practices, and gets better at it until you're real good at it. I think style comes from individual fighters, fighters that used what worked for them. It's those styles you are not familiar with that you have to be aware of.

Boxers usually get familiar with other fighters before their fight. Boxers have style and sometimes they have to change it up in order to confuse their opponent. Then there are those great fighters who see right through the image.

What do you remember most of all the masters you had the opportunity to train with?

I remember how they all trained the hard way to become who they were. I admire the masters who studied long enough and trained hard to the point of no longer envying other martial artists, but becoming one themselves. How in the old days it was about self-defense and developing a strong mind and body and spending lots of time alone training. The masters I remember eat and sleep martial arts, everything to them pertains to martial arts. Everything they do and say has something to do with either doing it the simplest way, healthiest way or being helpful in anyway. With Grandmaster Lara and Grandmaster Largusa, I had a small opportunity, only the amount of my pinky finger, of the physical aspect of training. I can say I learned more listening and watching them. I learned a lot from how Grandmaster Floro Villabrille and my Grandfather Graciano Lontayao Sr. observed practitioners demonstrate their art.

Please tell us a little bit about the philosophical and spiritual aspects of Villabrille-Lontayao system of Kali?

Let me start by saying my father's loyalty to the founder Grandmaster Floro Villabrille and to Grandmaster Ben T. Largusa who was responsible for breaking down the art of Kali move by move into a Kali system for teaching purposes, was at the highest respect any martial artist could ever have. He spent many years by their side dedicated in teaching the system the way he learned it and honoring them and to make it clear "never retiring from the system" he was devoted although apart physically always with them spiritually. My last conversation with my father regarding Martial Arts he asked if I heard anything from the Association. He passed away with his family by his bedside on March 25, 2012. Martial Artists from all different schools and Islands came to pay their last final respects, and upon his wishes he left this world in his red Kali vest holding his teaching command sticks. That night we honored his weapon (The Bahi) by passing it through the line with some performing their Halad (an expression of gratitude). The Bahi was passed starting with his grandchildren then to his students, to the Guro's and through his Professors, to Grandmaster Lara then to the family and ending with me for one last performance for him his sayau. To continue his legacy, my hand carved Bahi from The Island of Siquijor was passed down the line in reverse for the blessing of a new era. His final day of rest, his oldest instructors came out as if they came onto the floor one last time together the air was still, and drizzle was coming down through the sunlight. The movements were slow; the smiles were of peace as they said their last good bye to a good friend. The Organization then lined up, said the Orascion (prayer) and saluted with a pause one last time to our great teacher Prof. Graciano "Greg" Lontayao Jr.

How different from other Martial arts styles do you see the principles and concepts of Kali?

Well there is the principle of De Cadena (unbroken rhythm) which, to some, has to be reminded in practice because it takes listening and feeling. The way it's developed in Kali is through drills that exercise rhythm and timing through the coordination of strikes and footwork at the same time to the sound of the beats. Once you have learned to move having rhythm and timing behind your footwork and strikes you can easily speed up your movements and when each move flows into another, gaining momentum there is now continuity and you also learn how to interrupt it too. You can interrupt by knowing your opponent's attacks are continuing so you have to act fast by intercepting the path and jam the strike by applying checks and rechecks; moving is your parry, your check is your strike. How music is related to Kali is in the dance. When you dance you want to move around use your hands and feet, move freely in and out and move in half circles up or down, shuffle your feet, pivot your feet and stomp your feet, be soft but then yet hard and be hard but then yet soft. Offense becomes defense and defense becomes offense. Another principle is using "thought to reach the key to add to contact."

Do you think that Kali in the west has "caught up" with the technical level in the Philippines?

I've seen Filipino Martial Arts in the Philippines on T.V and it looks alive and well and very active. The Kali that I know here in the west carries on and has much respect for the Philippines for that is

ESCRIMA MASTERS

where the Chieftain Lapu Lapu and his people defended themselves with their fighting skills against the Spanish Invaders. If all Filipino Martial Arts continue to promote what our teachers have passed on the fighting arts of the Philippines and Indonesia it will be preserved and protected and its land will always represent a proud culture.

Arnis is nowadays often referred to as a sport. Would you agree with this definition?

I could agree to a certain extent, if it represents well and not become something that does not require much skill and anyone off the street could use a weapon and swing away only to score as much points in a time frame no matter how he/she does it, if it takes two strikes and rushing in to be the winner then anyone can do that especially when you have head gear on for protection. If Kali and Arnis just like anything else is going to be in competition like other sports it takes time to develop. It takes discipline, respect, conditioning, stamina and strength, basic fundamentals, balance, technique, practice and most of all sportsmanship. If you don't understand why, then it's not Martial Arts you are representing. In the old days, the more experienced fighter would have no respect for those who show off. Kali to me is more art and it's beyond that too. The beauty of the art is in your expression. Kali is a fighting art and if you learn the principles and theories the way it's taught your movements have more definition and meaning. It takes more than external abilities but also internal abilities and spiritual guidance to bring out everything. That's why the art is deadly and now practiced only to uphold its principles, philosophies and its culture.

Do you feel that you still have further to go in your studies of the art?

I remember growing up and demonstrating the art of Kali for Grandmasters and Masters of so many different styles and how they had reached that age that it was no longer necessary for them to show. I see myself as half their age. My place is still on the floor not up front watching as they did. I will never forget how it is to be in the line. All of my teachers are no longer on the floor with me and I can just fall back in line. They are only with me in spirit now and their teaching continues.

How do you remember your father and his contribution to the art of Kali?

I will start with my father and the student. He promoted when he saw improvement and progress. His promotions were usually announced on a certain month or year because being promoted is an accomplishment that deserves recognition for those individuals and he always included family and other instructors and his teachers to witness. Promotions required testing, sometimes testing was a surprise. He would say every class was a test. He also taught students not to ask to be promoted, and when they were promoted not to question why. It shows disrespect to you, the martial arts, and the teacher. My father based his promotions on attitude, respect, dedication, time and patience, and friendship among others and fellow classmates. He taught to acknowledge his teachers and instructors and also the different styles he had learned. He taught his students to respect what other styles have to offer and learn what can be useful. He opened Martial Art schools at home and commercially, in clubhouses, recreation centers and even church halls. His home schools gave his students a closer connection to him. His students reached levels that eventually enabled them to start assisting him. In time they proved worthy of becoming instructors themselves. The students felt very confident in the skills and knowledge they now possessed, so my father gave them the blessing to continue on their own and through them his teaching began to branch out. They learned that teaching is not easy. His instructors developed character and became unique individuals with their own unique style, not one being the same. His demonstrations took place at a variety of different locations and events such as, universities, community colleges, high schools, elementary schools, sports events, carnivals, community festivals, cultural festivals, city halls, art museums, Chinese New Year parades, Hawaiian clubs, Ho'olau'leas, Martial Art schools, tournaments and seminars. He also contributed to the Black Belt Magazine and Inside Kung-fu Magazine. My father also organized dinner banquets and entertainment to honor the Grandmaster and Master and brought other martial art schools together to honor his teachers. One of these events was the idea of Ron Smith, a student of my father. It took place on June 18, 1993, and was appropriately named the Living Treasures of the Filipino Martial Arts. I remember how good my father was. One time he and I were demonstrating and I hit the stick out of his hand and I swear I seen the stick come out of his hand and fall to the ground and bounced back in his hand and he just continued striking me.

Do you have any general advice you would like to pass on to practitioners in general?

I would say always remember there is more to learn. Be open-minded when it comes to differences and opinions. How one person sees it is how that person learned to understand it more than others. Like my teachers would say "that's good." Martial Arts in general should have good listeners and be friendly and help one another. Don't let your practice become stagnant, you can always improve on what you already know. This will help you understand the simplest things. Observe, absorb and digest.

Some people think going to the Philippines to really progress in the art is highly necessary. Do you share this point of view?

I can see for some practitioners they would feel it be necessary. If they feel they can progress seek and find something to improve their skills, satisfy their curiosity and exchange or challenge their skills then that's good. Some have to see for themselves. I've seen for myself. I didn't ask; I didn't seek. I made a mistake one night on the Island of Siquijor. My father asked me to get my Uncle Joe because he needed help with some lighting out on the patio. So I ran to the small hut behind the main house where he lived. The hut had only one wall and a roof made of bamboo covered with coconut tree palms and a cot made out of bamboo. The bamboo and the wood was cut in the month of December to withstand typhoons. Anyways, I was excited and in a hurry, I ran towards him and didn't notice him sleeping. All I said was "Uncle Joe" and before I could finish his name, he already had his stick in hand and on his feet. I didn't even realize what had happened, and as if it was nothing he just went right away to help my father. I don't know why now it has occurred to me that in one motion he grabbed the stick and got up as if he had done that before, it was fast. I remember him giving me handmade swimming goggles and a

ESCRIMA MASTERS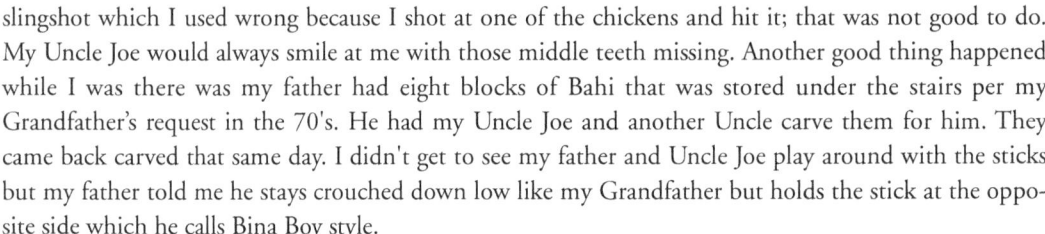

slingshot which I used wrong because I shot at one of the chickens and hit it; that was not good to do. My Uncle Joe would always smile at me with those middle teeth missing. Another good thing happened while I was there was my father had eight blocks of Bahi that was stored under the stairs per my Grandfather's request in the 70's. He had my Uncle Joe and another Uncle carve them for him. They came back carved that same day. I didn't get to see my father and Uncle Joe play around with the sticks but my father told me he stays crouched down low like my Grandfather but holds the stick at the opposite side which he calls Bina Boy style.

What are the aspects you think western practitioners advantage their Philippines counterpart?

Well I really can't say because I haven't been to the Philippines but two times, once in the early 80's and again in the early 90's. There is a diverse group of people who are interested in the Filipino Martial Arts and are unable to travel to the Philippines to study it. I maybe wrong, but I would think western practitioners have opportunities to learn from a variety of schools that offer more than one style, or academies of different martial arts under one roof.

What would you say to someone who is interested in starting to learn Kali?

The first thing you learn is how to listen. Be patient, give yourself time, don't get discouraged.

Relax don't try so hard, learn and practice at home. It's like going to the gym the first night you feel pain but in this case you feel uncoordinated, out of shape and overwhelmed and turning to face in different directions will confuse you. Everything starts with the basics and once you get the ball rolling you can improve and you will not even notice that you learned so much in your first two hours. You forget about life outside of Kali class, because it gets that challenging. Remember the moment you set foot through the door your training begins. Go early to class and use the time to practice and ask questions. When it's time to line up, don't drag your feet like your getting out of bed. Find your place and be ready, always be ready. Move on the sound of command not after the sound but with the sound, train to have agility second to the cat and have reflexes sharp as a razor.

What do you see as the most important attributes of a student?

A student's attitude reflects on how much he has learned and what his teacher has taught him. Our philosophy behind the Orascion (prayer or meditation) before class begins and at the end of class with our eyes closed. One is reminded that you also close your eyes to the outside world so you don't bring it into class and use dangerous sharp weapons that may hurt or injure a classmate intentionally, and we close our eyes at the end of class so we keep what we have practiced on the floor and "never have to speak of it or use it outside of class." This teaches you respect for the arts. It's important that a student not only see the physical aspects of martial arts but also the spiritual aspect of the martial arts so he/she sees the whole picture.

It's important that a student of Martial arts learns that it's more than fighting and not about hurting others. It's important they see that by training the mind and body they can accomplish what goals they set for themselves. There should be no conflict about one style or art being better than the other, one person learning longer than another, one person claiming to have learned more than another, or one claiming he will out rank the other. You are taught rank isn't important, but attitude and ones interest in learning martial arts are. Wanting to become higher rank then another was never encouraged. There should never be a student telling his teacher anything about another student.

What are your thoughts on the future of the art?

The future of Kali is in good hands. It has been broken down and turned into a system that everyone can experience and learn. The principles and theories have been written, the art has been demonstrated and it has established a seat in the Martial Arts category by well-recognized true Martial Artist. The Filipino fighting arts will prevail because the Islands have a proud culture to preserve. Kali is unique, its fluent movements take rhythmic feeling to develop continuity within, and it could be disguised in dance. If the student and his teacher always have the respect for one another, there is the blessing to carry on. Good teachers allow students to go out on their own and sometimes it shows when a student is capable of not limiting themselves have no boundaries have no end.

Here reads a Christmas greeting card I received after having traveled to Germany to conduct a Kali seminar.

Dear Sean,

I'm glad to hear that you had a wonderful trip to Germany and a joyful visit there. I am also pleased to know that the seminar proved to be successful there. This is a good start, and you and your Dad will be expecting more invitations here on. It's time and long overdue that someone is finally spreading Kali in its true style or form which the Grandmaster founded and as taught by the Largusa School of Kali. Kali needs to be spread nationally and internationally and I'm pleased that you and your Dad are starting to do it. Hang in there and keep up the good work. Enjoy the season's holidays!

Peace & Love always,
Your God-father,
Ben T. Largusa
Grandmaster

CHRIS RICKETTS

KALI ILUSTRISIMO – THE ORIGINAL WAY

Christopher Ricketts was a senior student of the late great Antonio "Tatang" Ilustrisimo for almost 25 years. As a master of Kali Ilustrisimo, he is recognized as one of the leading authorities on the field. The style, named after "Tatang" Ilustrisimo, is based on the traditional Filipino sword fighting methods and refined by Antonio Ilustrisimo's vast personal experience in challenge matches. The art of Kali Ilustrisimo hails from Cebu, Philippines, where martial arts still are considered a matter of life-and-death survival—rather than a sport or science—and offer a powerful, flexible, dynamic, and effective fighting style.

Master Ricketts is the founder and Chief Instructor of Bakbakan International, a highly respected and leading martial arts organization. Now based in California, Master Ricketts hopes to make Kali Ilustrisimo more easily accessible in the U.S. and around the world to those who wish to study this highly effective and unique Filipino art.

How long have you been practicing martial arts?

My initial formal training began in 1963 at the age of 8. From that point on, I have been on a constant, full time martial art journey and have never stopped. Because the Philippines is an ancient cross roads of many cultures, I have the fortunate opportunity to practice numerous fine arts in their pure form.

I began training in Kali Ilustrisimo jn 1984 until Tatang Ilustrisimo's passing in 1997. Other Filipino martial arts training included the Rapillon style of Mang Sciano Cleope. In 1969, I was teaching his son, Edgar Cleope. His father was a well-known eskrimador from the Quezon province of the Philippines. I also trained with Philippine martial arts legend Master Doc Lengson in the Karate Arnis Federation of the Philippines (KAFEPHIL) style from 1968 until Doc died. I also was the training partner for Tony Diego and the late Edgar Sulite. It was through our constant sparring experimentation that he came up with the basis for the original Lameco Eskrima sparring curriculum.

ESCRIMA MASTERS

Along the way, I have picked up a few teaching credentials, including Kali Ilustrisimo, Ngo Cho Kuen (Five Ancestor Fist), and Sagasa Filipino Kickboxing. I also am a professional boxing trainer. At one stage, I had a full stable of pro boxers, with some making it into the top 10 of their weight class.

What were the teaching methods like?

A true practitioner of Kali Ilustrisimo will have totally instinctive reaction, with no set pattern. Tatang never responded the same way to the same angle of attack. His movements were so natural and a wonder to behold.

Tatang did not teach you in the traditional sense. If I simulated an attack angle against him, he would respond instinctively, usually at a level that was very painful as he frequently would actually be hitting me. It was up to you to understand and absorb the techniques he used. In the old days, the five pillars (Tony Diego, Yuli Romo, Rey Galang, Edgar Sulite, and I) would draw straws to see who would have the painful honor to simulate the attack against Ilustrisimo, while the others would observe and take notes. There was no progression, forms, or structure. The main structures and progressions being taught to the public these days are based on individual interpretations of the original five pillars of Kali Ilustrisimo.

Do you have a particularly memorable training experience?

There are so many. Very few had the privilege to spar Tatang on a regular basis as I did, but there is one occasion I will not soon forget. In general, Tatang was a respectful gentleman. However, on this particular day I kept telling him that he was not able to hit me. I was doing this in order to see how the old man would press his attack and possibly reveal some new strategies and techniques; a sacrifice so to speak. Immediately, Tatang stood up and began striking me in the head. He quickly feinted left, and then suddenly struck me in the right eye with an inside De Cadena attack. Tatang struck me so hard I actually believed he had knocked my eyeball out and so I dropped to the ground in search of my eyeball!

When I realized my eye was still intact, I stood up and Tatang asked if I was okay. When I said I was fine, without hesitation, he continued his barrage of attacks upon me. Tatang always was willing to fight to the end, even in training sessions. Now that he has gone, even the painful memories have become fond memories.

How has your perception of the art and training in kali developed over the years?

Throughout the years training under Tatang, up until his death in 1997, I was constantly learning, dissecting, experimenting, analyzing, and observing his movements. I was primarily in an "absorbing mode." After Tatang's death, I continued to do the same with the technical material I had retained. Now I have come full circle back to his original techniques: direct, uncomplicated, and effective. When I went back and reviewed the hundreds of hours of film archives on Tatang, it confirmed that I am on the right path—and still in wonder of my teacher's abilities.

Do you think there still is a "pure" system of Kali and Escrima, or we are going to a more "mixed" approach?

I am aware of schools that are very pure and traditional and I am aware of schools that are open-minded and experimental. Although there is a trend in the "mixed" approach, both schools of thought always will exist. Some people can make this "mix" work…others just repeat without a real sense.

What are the major changes in the arts since you began training?

When I was starting, there was no training gear for our stick and empty hand sparring. There was a lot less margin for error or experimentation. Nowadays, we have protective gear and other helps to our training. We can make a mistake in training safely, without getting a permanent injury. This is good because it allows us to experiment with things and techniques without getting seriously hurt.

How do you think a practitioner can increase his or her understanding of the spiritual aspects of the arts?

The opportunity to connect to the spiritual side of the arts is always present. It is just a matter of choice and desire for practitioner. I would suggest, however, that they be clear of their purpose and intentions before embarking in this direction.

Do you think that Filipino Arts in the West has caught up to the level of the Philipines?

That is a difficult question to answer because the Philippines is a land literally divided by thousands of islands. The country also is divided traditionally, with many languages, dialects, ethnicities, religions, barangays, cities, towns, villages and so forth. Within this type of environment, there exist many forms of the Filipino warrior arts that have not been exposed even in Manila, let alone the West. Also, keep in mind that there are areas of the Philippines that have been war zones for many generations for political and religious reasons. These conditions call for less theory and more realism. Theory is good…but theory and practice is much better.

ESCRIMA MASTERS

Are martial arts a sport or a way of life?

For some it is a sport, for some it is a way of life, and for others it is both. Martial arts have a little bit of everything for all to enjoy. We are not in war times, so there is no reason to think in terms of killing, but we have to be serious in our training and differentiate between play and real fighting.

Do you think it helps students to train with weapons?

More understanding of all possible factors in the equation of combat is always a plus. Therefore, I believe that weaponry training is a very big help for any martial artists, regardless of style.

Who would you like to have trained with that you have not, and why?

Naturally, I would have liked to continue training under my primary teacher,

Ilustrisimo, as he never ceased to amaze me. I also would have liked to have sparred with Masters Johnny Chiuten, Doc Lengson, and Lito Vito in their prime. These were some of the finest empty hands fighters I have seen. They were capable of executing traditional kung fu techniques in a textbook manner in real fighting encounters. It was beautiful to watch.

What keeps you motivated to train after all these years?

The friendships I have developed over the years.

Do you think no-holds-barred events bring positive or negative aspects to the martial arts?

The sport is good for shedding light on many perspectives of engagement. I just hope that important values and traditions, such as respect, honor, humility, integrity, and self-discipline survive the rapid commercial growth.

Do you have any general advice to pass on?

Be honest and objective with yourself. Keep you ego in check. Practice humility, respect, honor, integrity, and self-disclpline.

What are your thoughts on the future of Kali Ilustrisimo and Filipino martial arts?

I am concerned with the preservation of all the arts in their purest form. Personally, my main concern is with Kali Ilustrisimo. After the death of Tatang, many people suddenly appeared claiming to represent Kali Ilustrisimo. These people mainly are good at talking and making theories. However, this is not enough if you are claiming to be a true authority on the subject. You also must practice Tatang's real techniques and be able to apply them. As much as I would like to personally and physically stop these pretenders, my objective now is to be a bastion of Tatang's authentic methods. Many people are good at talking, but when it comes to sparring, they either decline or perform very badly. Unfortunately, there are people exploiting the Ilustrisimo name and actually are teaching their own personal vision. When teaching, you must make the distinction between your version and the original. If people are not honest and this keeps up, the art will continue to be watered down and may eventually be lost completely.

Since the passing of Tatang, there many people have proclaimed publicly that they were "certified" by Tatang. There are all manners of scenarios: some spent a week, a month or just took a photo with Tatang to become "certified." There are very few credible martial arts that will consider certifying anyone with even two years of dedicated training, let alone two weeks. There is even a story of people helping Tatang with his medical bills in his twilight years and being awarded certification for their help.

There always will be unscrupulous people who will say anything to become "known" in the world of martial arts, even at the expense of the art. Because of these facts, my main focus now is concentration on Tatang's original core techniques, the roots of his system, which I always differentiate from drills developed by any one of the five pillars. Who is to say what is original and what is not? On top of the fact that I was one of his most physically dedicated students, the hundreds of hours of Tatang's film archives that I have of him in action speak for themselves. I have the finest Ilustrisimo archives in the world with him in action and being interviewed.

The majority of what is being pushed today as Kali Ilustrisimo never was done by Tatang. Let your eyes be the judge by viewing the archives. Being one of the five pillars of Kali Ilustrisimo and spending countless hours with Tatang, I take great offense at the actions of pretenders. I have dedicated a good portion of my life to this art. It is a part of me. Regardless of these facts, I always will attempt to settle misunderstandings as a gentleman, first and foremost. However, if this course of action fails, I will not hesitate to settle it as an Eskrimador. It is, after all, the "Warrior Arts" and not the "Verbal Debating Arts." I have full confidence in the actual techniques Tatang has passed on to me. Many are all theory and no practice. I am not one of them.

TONY SOMERA

A HIGHER CALLING

FEW ARE THE CHOSEN ONES FORTUNATE ENOUGH TO BE CLOSE TO LEGENDARY NAMES OF THE MARTIAL ARTS WORLD. EVEN FEWER INDIVIDUALS HAVE THE PRIVILEGE OF SHARING THEIR LIVES WITH GREAT MASTERS, IN-AND-OUT OF THE TRAINING HALL, LEARNING FROM THEIR EXPERIENCES, AND LISTENING EVERYDAY TO A WEALTH OF WISDOM AND KNOWLEDGE ONLY GATHERED BY A HANDFUL OF MARTIAL ARTS INSTRUCTORS. MASTER TONY SOMERA WAS ONE OF THE FEW. HE SPENT MANY YEARS OF HIS LIFE WITH THE LATE GRANDMASTER LEO GIRON. GRANDMASTER GIRON SELECTED SOMERA TO BECOME THE HEIR OF HIS SYSTEM, AND THE RELATIONSHIP BOTH MEN SHARED UNTIL THE DAY GIRON PASSED AWAY WAS UNIQUE. THEIR BONDING WAS BEYOND MARTIAL ARTS — THEIR RELATIONSHIP WAS LIKE A FATHER AND SON. TONY SOMERA WAS THE ONLY PERSON EVER TO BE PROMOTED TO THE RANK OF MASTER AND THEN GRAND MASTER BY THE LATE GRAND MASTER EMERITUS LEO M. GIRON.

How long have you been practicing the martial arts?
I began when I was nine. This would be almost 40 years ago.

How many styles of escrima or other methods have you trained in?
In 1976, I started my escrima training with Gilbert Tino, a master in the decuerdas system. But that would only last for about six months. After questioning my father about Filipino martial arts, my father finally directed me to go and see my Uncle Leo (Leo Giron). My father had referred to Leo Giron as my uncle because my father and Giron belonged to the same Filipino fraternal order and one of the strongest Filipino lodges … the Legionarios Del Trabajo in America.

I remember that a friend and karate student of mine was also researching Filipino arts. One day we decided to go to visit Uncle Leo. I remember the first day of training with him. We got out of our car and walked toward Uncle Leo's house. There he was watering his front lawn before class had begun. Uncle Leo looked up at me and said, "You have grown since last time I have seen you. How are your mom and dad?" As we went to the backyard, all I could remember is that he was trying to catch up on

my life and what I have been doing. He also talked about farming and how my mom and dad were very hard workers. That whole evening during class as I watched other young students "play" (as Uncle Leo would referred training too). I was jumping at the correct time to ask permission to "play" with him. I felt like he was interviewing me for a job. Finally, almost at the end of class, he asked me if I would like to play. By that time, the class was just about over, and he said to come back to the next class on Wednesday. I returned that next Wednesday and started my formal training in Giron arnis escrima.

Tell us some interesting stories of your early days in martial arts training with grandmaster Leo Giron.

One time grandmaster Giron and I went to visit a local martial art supply store in Stockton, California. At the time there was an escrima class going on in the back room, and Giron wanted to visit the teacher. In the meantime, we were looking at the different martial art supplies. Of course, the rattan sticks caught the grandmaster's eye. The sales person said, "I noticed you are looking at the escrima sticks." The grandmaster replied, "Yes, is that what you call them?" The sales person said that these were special combat fighting weapons that are used for a style called larga mano. Well, the grandmaster perked up and said, "Larga Mano?" The sales person said yes, adding that this is the style of Leo Giron and that he was his teacher. The grandmaster looked at me with a smile and said, "Who is this Leo Giron?" The sales person said he is the father of larga mano in America and then he went on to explain the larga mano system. It was like watching the fox in a hen house. Eventually, the guro from the school came out to greet grandmaster Giron. When he walked out, he turned to the sales person and said, "This is grandmaster Leo Giron." I think the sales person was a little embarrassed. We all had a big laugh and after enjoyed causal conversation.

With all the technical changes during the last 30 years, do you think there are still pure styles of escrima or kali?

A; I can only speak of our system of escrima because I have not trained enough in the art of kali. So, having said that, I feel strongly that our system of escrima is still pure. The only things that have changed have been the different applications against the different types of weapons and aggressive opponents. As a second-generation escrima-dor, I have the opportunity to apply the different playing techniques in many different and exciting ways. The basic fundamentals are the same and should never change.

How do you see Filipino martial arts in America at the present time?

I feel that this is a great time in history for Filipino martial arts in America. The Filipino arts are growing. As more Americans explore the arts, they will experience and see the effectiveness the Filipino martial arts have to offer. Not only in the physical application of defensive protection but also in the rich Filipino culture and history. In the first half of the 1900s, Filipinos were the backbone of agriculture development in America. In the early 1900s, California — and in particular Stockton — had the greatest population of Filipino's. As a result, Stockton received the name "Little Manila."

Does it enhance the empty hand aspect of the art to train with weapons?

Yes, but you need to understand — as a teacher or student — the role the weapon will play in a confrontation, along with the role that empty hands will have as the extension of the weapon. In the Giron

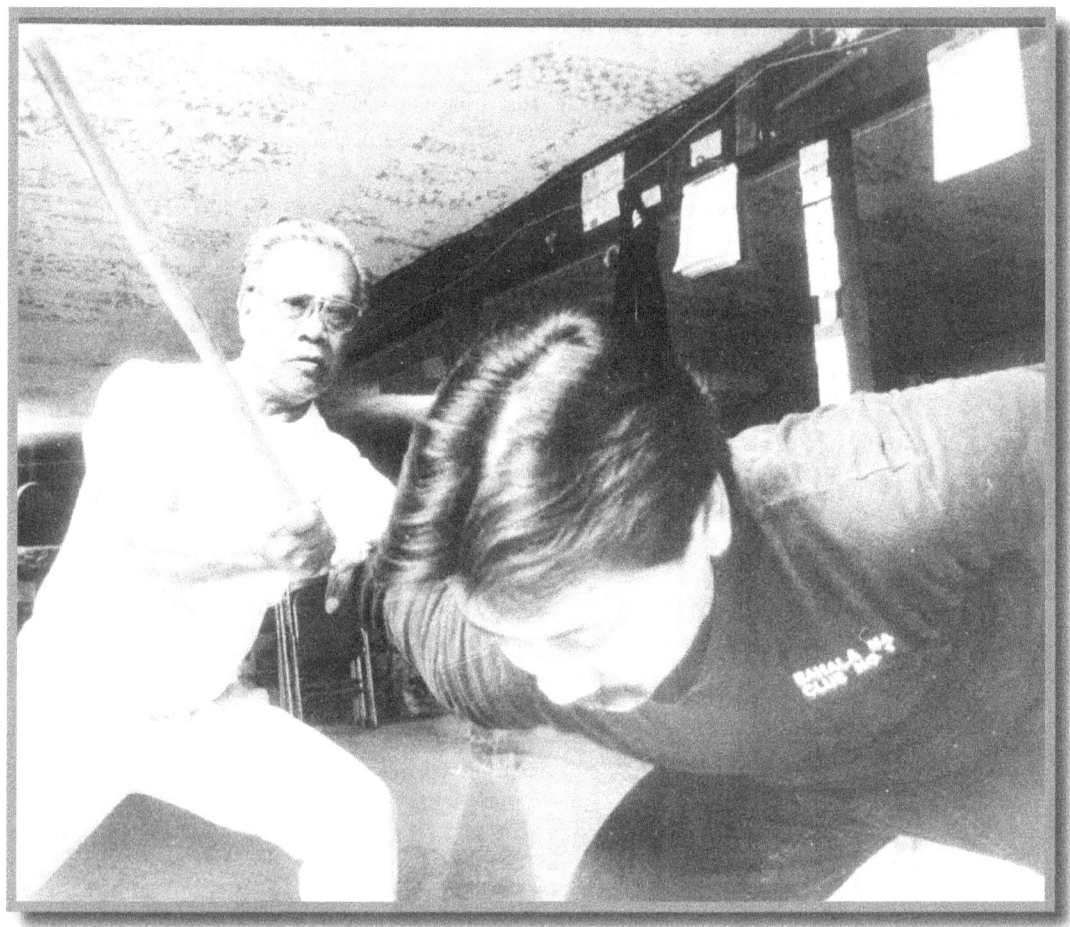

system, we start training the student first with the weapon and then apply the same knowledge to the empty-hand application. I have found that the weapon training has enhanced the empty hand application and in most cases will increase your hand speed and accuracy.

What is your opinion about mixing escrima styles?

Mixing escrima systems can be confusing for everyone. It has been the teachings of grandmaster Giron that learning other escrima styles can help you to understand the Filipino arts and see the big picture. But, as a teacher or student of the Filipino arts, you must always identify with the styles you are playing. Meaning that if you are teaching a certain style of escrima, you must always let your students know what style you are now teaching. You must also acknowledge the styles and masters of those systems.

As for effectiveness, it can be like mixing oil and vinegar. On the other hand, mixing styles can prove to be an effective combination that is quite deadly.

How can a practitioner increase his understanding of the spiritual aspect of the art?

Certainly, if you are practicing an art, you are already studying the spiritual aspect of the art. From the time you step on the floor to train you begin to sense or pick up certain characteristics of your teacher and fellow students. Watch what is taking place around you as you train. Be aware of how your teacher is teaching the art; be aware of how you and your fellow students demonstrate the art. Do your research and ask questions. Try to learn more about your art's history and culture and by all means ask your teacher questions.

What are your thoughts on the future of the arts?

We are in a time of history that is so very important. With many — if not all — of the masters that have paved the way for us passing away, our generation will now need to set the standards for the next generation of practitioners. We must continue to carry on the arts of our forefathers. We must be the ones that will teach and tell the stories of the ancient ones. The stories of the manongs that were experts in the Filipino arts that came to this country to seek a better opportunity and to have a better life. We must never forget all of the wonderful experiences that we had shared with them so that our experiences will be those that will follow in tracing our footsteps. The most wonderful gift I can give will be the teachings of my teacher to the next generation of practitioners so that our forefather's hardships that they had to endure will not be in vain.

EDGAR G. SULITE

THE LEGACY OF STEEL

He was a unique individual who belonged to that special group of people who, with their inner power and charisma, touch the lives of many others. Punong Guro Edgar Sulite was born on September 25, 1957, in Tacloban City on the Philippine island of Leyte. He was raised in a family of martial artists. His father, Hilacrio Sulite, was a professional boxer and arnis expert, as well as a U.S. Army veteran, and his brother, Hilacrio Jr., was a karate expert. During his childhood, Edgar witnessed the deadly Filipino martial arts in actual combat because brawls between arnis experts were common in his rural province. He came to both know and admire the men behind the art.

At the age of eight Edgar's father began teaching him Western boxing and then, at 12, arnis. It was common for Edgar to be battered on his hands and feet to correct technical mistakes in training; this was the traditional way. This method, although cruel, helped him to build resistance to pain and the courage to persevere through adversity. While simultaneously training under his father and coming to master the family system known as sulite repelon, Edgar expanded his skill by training with other masters and grandmasters all across the Philippine Islands.

His family moved to Ozamis when his father was transferred there, and Edgar was able to finish his bachelor of arts in economics from Misamis University. Taking advantage of residing in the city, Edgar furthered his knowledge by studying under different arnis masters. Some of his instructors were Grandmaster Antonio Illustrisimo of Bag-on Bantayan, founder of kali illustrisimo; Leo Gaje, pekiti tirsia inventor; Jose Caballero, originator of de Campo uno-dos-tres; and Jesus Abella, grandmaster of modernos largos. Edgar devoted the first third of his life to the study of these traditional combat systems and their masters. This discipline of mind and body transformed him from an awkward youth to the refined physical embodiment of technical perfection he was to become.

Reaching adulthood, Edgar, now know as "Punong Guro Sulite," founded the lameco system of arnis, which describes the different kali methods of largo, medio, and corto. Punong Guro Sulite didn't create a new system simply to become a grandmaster, as such. His intention in creating lameco eskrima was to properly organize, in a

ESCRIMA MASTERS

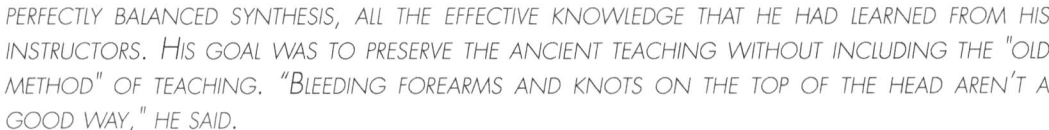

PERFECTLY BALANCED SYNTHESIS, ALL THE EFFECTIVE KNOWLEDGE THAT HE HAD LEARNED FROM HIS INSTRUCTORS. HIS GOAL WAS TO PRESERVE THE ANCIENT TEACHING WITHOUT INCLUDING THE "OLD METHOD" OF TEACHING. "BLEEDING FOREARMS AND KNOTS ON THE TOP OF THE HEAD AREN'T A GOOD WAY," HE SAID.

WHEN ASKED HOW HE PLANNED TO PRESERVE THE ANCESTRAL TEACHINGS, HE ANSWERED, "I HAVE SYSTEMATIZED AND PRESENTED THE ARTS IN A MODERN CONTEXT EASILY "ASSIMILABLE" THROUGH A SYNTHESIS OF MULTIPLE EFFECTIVE SYSTEMS. STUDENTS FROM ALL OVER THE WORLD WERE FORTUNATE ENOUGH TO TRAIN UNDER PUNONG GURO SULITE AND RECEIVE BOTH THE ANCIENT KNOWLEDGE AND THE OLD TRADITIONS OF THE FILIPINO ARTS OF ESKRIMA, ARNIS, AND KALI. HE WAS A TRUE PIONEER WHO HELPED BRING THESE ARTS OUT OF THE DARKEST JUNGLES INTO THE LIGHT OF THE MODERN DAY MARTIAL ARTS SPECTRUM.

THE FOLLOWING INTERVIEW, ARRANGED BY DAN INOSANTO, TOOK PLACE IN 1990, IN THE LIVING ROOM OF THAI BOXING MASTER CHAI SIRISUTE'S HOUSE IN TORRANCE, CALIFORNIA. THIS WAS LONG BEFORE GURO SULITE'S SKILL AND KNOWLEDGE GENERALLY WERE KNOWN. IT WAS FOLLOWED BY TWO STRAIGHT HOURS OF STICK TWIRLING, WEAPON DISARMS, JOINT LOCKS, LETHAL KNIFE TECHNIQUES, AND POWERFUL INSIGHTS ON THE COMBATIVE ASPECTS OF ARNIS. I NEVER WILL FORGET THAT FIRST "SPECIAL OCCASION" OF BEING BATTERED WITH SUCH AMAZING SKILL, PRECISION, AND SPEED.

BEFORE LEAVING THIS WORLD TO PURSUE HIGHER GOALS, PUNONG GURO SULITE LEFT WITH US HIS LEGACY OF STEEL.

Kali, eskrima, and arnis all are names for the Filipino martial arts. Which one is correct?

In Mindanao, kali was the term used, but it doesn't mean that it is the only one. In fact, the three names mean the same. My first name is Edgar, the middle name is Gerez, and my last name is Sulite. The three of them describe the same person. They are three different names to describe the same art. We must remember that, according to the region where you live, the term changes and others apply such as estocada, pagkalikali, etc.

Your art does not focus on "flashy" demonstration techniques. Why is that?

I use some techniques for demonstrations. We have to have some of these if you want to give impressive demos, but you're right, my system, what I really teach, is not meant for show. It is for real combat. Whatever techniques that don't fit into this principle are discarded immediately.

You have been living in the USA since 1989 and visited other countries such as Germany, Australia, New Zealand, etc. What would be your advice to these practitioners? What did you think of the art as it is practiced there?

First, there are some people who only have been in a few seminars and have credentials to teach. This is wrong. It doesn't matter who is the one that addressed those certifications. This is not good for the art, or for the instructor giving those credentials out. Their reputation and credibility are on the line. On

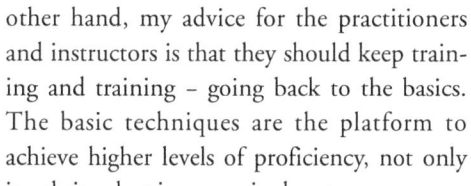

other hand, my advice for the practitioners and instructors is that they should keep training and training – going back to the basics. The basic techniques are the platform to achieve higher levels of proficiency, not only in eskrima but in every single art.

What differences did you notice between the way the art is practiced in the Philippines and the way it is taught and practiced in the U.S.A or Europe?

I can't talk about every country since I don't know, but I guess that the major difference is the mentality the art is practiced with. This changes the whole perception and view of it. It is very different when you practice eskrima for fighting for real and to protect your life than if you train just for fun or enjoy a physical activity. Back in the Philippines, we used certain methods that wouldn't fit the western mentality. I could run out students right away.

What's your view on arnis sport tournaments?

They are okay, but a lot of important things can be missing. If we really hit the hand holding the weapon, in most situations, the fight is going to be over. But in a tournament, this action is not that relevant. The environment and experience that you can get from a tournament can be deceiving if you don't know how to properly read what you're doing. This is the reason why in the Philippines we have two different kind of tournaments: with safety equipment and without it.

Can you talk about the spiritual aspects of the Filipino arts?

Of course there are religious aspects involved in the art. The Filipino people believe in God and the Muslims in Allah. These are different conceptions of a higher being. But it is only when you have reached a high level of physical proficiency that your instructor introduces you into the spiritual levels. Traditionally, it is your teacher who gives you an oracion for you to pray.

Would you like to add anything?

Yes, I would like to say that the art have to be practiced in the right way. Don't play with the art; give it the right credit. Develop the art of eskrima properly, with the right attitude and training, thinking about the real situations. Kali is not a game.

DARREN G. TIBON

ANGEL'S DISCIPLES

DARREN TIBON IS A DIRECT DISCIPLE OF ONE OF THE GREATEST MASTERS OF OUR GENERATION BUT WHAT HAS SOLIDIFIED HIS PLACE AMONG THE BEST "ESCRIMADORS" IS NOT JUST HIS TALENT TO PERFORM, BUT ALSO HIS WILLINGNESS TO SHARE WHAT HE HAS LEARNED WITH STUDENTS AROUND THE WORLD. GURO TIBON NOT ONLY WORKS CONTINUALLY TO PRESERVE AND PROMOTE HIS ART, BUT ALSO TO ADVANCE IT, BY INTRODUCING NEW INNOVATIVE APPROACHES TO TRAINING METHODOLOGY. HIS DIRECT, HUMOROUS, ENGAGING TEACHING STYLE HAS PARTICIPANTS – FROM BEGINNER TO ADVANCED – SMILING, LEARNING AND TRAINING HARDER THAN THEY EVER THOUGHT POSSIBLE. HE IS AN APPROACHABLE INSTRUCTOR, FULL OF EXCITEMENT AND JOY, AS HE SHARES THIS ANCIENT TREASURE WITH THE WORLD.

IN THIS REVEALING INTERVIEW, GURO TIBON TALKS ABOUT THE CREATION OF THE "ANGEL'S DISCIPLES" AND THE TIME SPENT WITH THE LEGENDARY GRANDMASTER ANGEL CABALES.

Would you please tell us a little bit about you?

I was born in 1962 on the South Side of Stockton, Ca. I am the youngest of five siblings in my family. My brother Eugene Tibon Jr., is the eldest and my sisters, Leslie, Regina and Jackie and myself. In 1966, we moved to the west side of Stockton where my father still lives today.

Is it true that your father was a boxer?

Yes. My father had boxed as an amateur when he was younger but influenza took him out of the fight game and put him in Bret Harte Hospital for a few years. When he got out he had to provide for a growing family. Dad joined up with Sensei Rodney Hu in the mid '60s. By the '70s, my Dad started training with the late GM Angel Cabales. My martial arts training began in the living room and backyard. that was the "gym". The neighborhood we moved into was predominantly white. As kids, we were picked on at school, walking to the park and even going to the store. That is where my Dad's combination of experience kicked in for us kids. Left jab, right cross, left uppercut or hook with various kicks and sweeps made for fast street-fighting techniques. This stuff worked and it saved us many times.

ESCRIMA MASTERS

Each teacher that my dad trained with, I also trained with. I trained with Sensei Rodney Hu from the mid '70s to mid '80s. Then with my cousin Joe Reasonable, who taught me "Serrada Escrima". After that, I trained with Gabriel Asuncion who also taught me Serrada Escrima and introduced me to Angel in 1983. My dad taught me Serrada Escrima to angle 5, my cousin Joe and Gabriel got me up to Angle 12 with lock and block and flow sparring. My official training with GM Angel Cabales started in 1985 and it was an art that I dedicated my life to.

What can you tell us about GM Angel Cabales? How did you get to meet him?

I was close friends with Vincent and Johnny Cabales, GM Angel's sons. I worked with Vincent Cabales at Century Metal Buildings from 1982-83. We fished and hunted together and we developed a friendship. I was asked to be he godfather to Vincent's daughter, Tiki. I was one of the best men at Vincent's wedding. Johnny and I used to lift weights together, he lived by my cousins house. I actually met Johnny when I was about 14 years old being in the neighborhood. Johnny, my cousin Larry, Tino and Daryl and I were all close, like brothers. Master Jerry Preciado and Master Gabriel Asuncion were also some of the neighborhood kids growing up together and were also Serrada students under GM Angel. The friendships from this neighborhood to the academy began. The keyhole shaped neighborhood I grew up in, there was one way in and one way out. There were kids of all ages. Many of my friends I grew up with and played sports with and went to the same schools together. We also trained marital arts, some at other martial art schools and some from the same martial arts school. I trained and would share what I learned from my father and from my "backyard" martial arts school. Charles, Kenny, Mark, Vincent and Roy were some of the lifelong friendships that I made growing up. We shared elementary, middle school and high schools and have memories of a lifetime, indeed, very similar to movies I have seen such as "The Sand Lot", "Stand by Me" and "The Wanderers" all combined into this one neighborhood.

Why did you get into the art of Escrima and the Filipino Martial Arts?

I am a second generation American born of Filipino decent. As a Tibon, it was important to understand my roots. My dad, my uncles and aunties shared with us all they knew from stories they heard from my great grandfather Marcos Tibon. I would visit him with my family when he was in a rest home. As early as I can remember, visiting great grandpa Marcos, he would put his hand on my stomach and then on my forehead, then open my hand and see the palm lines and say, "escrimador." Great grandpa Marcos' voice and his blessing stayed with me for life. The Tibon Family immigrated from Cebu, Lapu Lapu City, Philippines in 1906 and went to Oahu, Hawaii for a better life. Great grandpa

Marcos, who could speak several languages, was hired as an overseer at the Waialua Sugar Plantation, North Shore Oahu. On arrival to Oahu, great grandpa Marcos, great grandma Tamosa and three sons, Saturnino, Pastor and Francisco were very young children at the time. On Oahu, two daughters were born. My Auntie Enyon and Auntie Delores in 1914 and 1916. In 1920, the influenza epidemic had taken the life of great grandma Tamosa, leaving behind her three sons and two young daughters. With the position as an overseer in this era, people in these positions would often be challenged by other escrimadors. It was said that great grandpa Marcos had taken many challenges behind the old sugar mill and was never defeated. Before leaving the Phillipines, Great grandpa Marcos had killed many during such challenges.

After great grandma's death, the older sons and the two daughters set sail for California, landing in San Francisco. Great grandpa Marcos was said to have stayed behind and continued taking challenges, as if he had a death wish because he was distraught after losing his wife, but great grandpa kept winning his fights. He later connected back with the family in the San Joaquin Valley in Stockton, California. In books that I have read, it is documented that the Tibon Family was the first of 400 families to settle in the San Joaquin Valley. As more Filipino immigrants arrived in the area, it was also said that for female Filipino women in San Joaquin Valley, my two Aunties were only two of 8 female Filipino women in the entire area.

They were now in the land of opportunity, there for a better life. The City of Stockton had signs posted on store doors, restaurants and hotels, they read, "No Dogs, No Cats, No Filipinos." My great grandfather's youngest daughter, Dolores, was only 11 years old when she was kidnapped by a grand oriental. Great grandpa Marcos found his daughter but had taken lives in the process of getting her back. It is said great grandpa Marcos had to escape to Mexico for many years until the statute of limitations was up for his arrest. He was 50 years old when this happened. He created another life in Mexico

ESCRIMA MASTERS

and it was said that while in Mexico, he had several blade fights and survived them. He returned 20 years later to live the rest of his life in Stockton, Ca. He passed away in 1968 and is buried at the Harding Way Catholic Cemetery in Stockton, CA with his oldest son, Saturnino.

Many of great grandpa's kids and nephews are buried at this cemetery. He is only 50 yards away from the late GM Angel Cabales, my Grandmaster of the art of Serrada Escrima.

When did you start to train?

At the age of 18, I had some knowledge of Serrada Escrima from what my father taught me and with what I had learned training with my cousin, Joe Reasonable, along with my ongoing training with Goju Ryu with Sensei Rodney Hu. In speaking with my father, at this time, he had asked that one of his sons take up Filipino Martial Arts to keep it in the Tibon Family. Although I loved the Goju Ryu art, I also loved Serrada Escrima. My brother, Gene Tibon Jr. had already started his first school, Tibon's Goju Ryu Fighting Arts, and this is when I made my life commitment to Serrada Escrima.

After training a while with my cousin, Joe Reasonable, me and Gabriel Asuncion were both from karate backgrounds. Gabriel was an Advanced student under the GM Cabales. Gabriel and I trained together Serrada Escrima and I shared a Goju-Ryu form with him in exchange. This training with Gabriel Asuncion truly opened me up to Serrada Escrima with a passion and love for the art. GM Cabales was aware that I was training with Gabriel and, although I was working a second shift for a period of time, the day shift finally came up and I was able to start training directly with GM Cabales at his academy.

How was GM Cabales?

GM Angel Cabales was no ordinary man. He was small in stature but extremely fast and strong. He was extraordinary. When I started my training at the academy GM Cabales was aware that I had trained the twelve angles, lock and block and sparring, however, he started me at angle "one" and I am glad he did this. As I came up for rank for my Advanced Diploma this training came privately at GM Cabales' house. He had set up Sundays from 9:00 am to 12:00 noon as my private day with him. Sometimes I would leave at 9:00 p.m. at night but when he wanted you to learn Advanced or Masters levels he would work you until exhaustion and until he knew you could understand the art of Serrada and perform it to his expertise. After graduation of my Advanced Degree with GM Cabales, he asked me if I would like

to pursue my Masters training. He agreed to have it on the same day and the same time at his house. Midway through my Masters training, I got a call from John Cabales. There had been some trouble and he was concerned. John said, "I am going to be gone for a very long time or I am going to die, please watch over my dad, keep the art strong and do not let it die or get weak." I said, "I would do that anyways, don't worry about that John." John said to me, I want you to step in my position as if you are a son and I will tell my dad this and let him know this is what I would like. I will call him right now and tell him. A few minutes later I received a call from GM Cabales and he said, "I talked to Jonny... okay." GM Angel truly cared for this arrangement between him and his son Johnny. I felt it in the training I was getting, I felt it in the conversations with him and I felt it with the involvement that he included me in with business arrangements and with his other students. In my mid 20's my family at this time was with my wife, Darlene and my two young children, Desiree and Chez and my deep personal relationship with the late GM Cabales. There was a sentimental concern of what Angel truly wanted for the future of his art which was often shared with me and the promise I made to John Cabales. After graduating with my Masters Degree, the late GM's health started to decline and his diagnosis of cancer began to weaken him. Many of his students would set up meetings with him such as Mark Wiley, Anthony Davis, Graciella Casillas, Clift Stewart and Khalid Khan. GM Cabales would call me up and ask that I attend these meetings. Angel would often call me to help teach some of his advanced students and students training for their Masters Degree. I considered this a privilege. GM Angel Cabales passed away on March 3, 1991. My teacher was gone.

How it was the situation after the GM passing?

After Angel passed away, I had a few private students that I had been teaching that were actual students of GM Angel at the academy. These students GM Angel had paired up with me and had asked if

ESCRIMA MASTERS

they could continue their training with me. A few months passed by and a good friend and fellow student, Master Jerry Preciado gave me a call. He had been working on a few properties that Gong Lee, the owner of the academy where GM Angel had taught since 1966. Gong Lee was a very friendly man that used to visit the class and say hello to GM Angel. He would sit down with his wife with a big smile on his face and watch all of us train. He would talk to us and say, "you guys move like Bruce Lee", in laughter. He had told Jerry that he noticed a lot of the students he used to see did not come around any more and asked if he was interested in a Sunday or Thursday spot at the hall. Master Jerry Preciado asked me if I wanted to open a day and I said: "let's do it". June 28, 1991, Angels Disciples Escrima Association was established. This school lasted until 2014 and, though I do not run a class at Gong Lee's Hall any longer, I have affiliate schools. "Angels Disciples" has students throughout the country and the world training "Angels Disciples Serrada Escrima".

You did get together with your brother Gene Tibon and did great things to honor the old masters. What can you tell us about it?

In 2006, my brother Gene Tibon Jr., while visiting my mother in the hospital, asked me if I would be interested in coordinating Stick Fighting with Disney Martial Arts Festival. I had a lot of experience with tournaments at this time. The Stockton Coalition and various other groups that ran FMA Stick Fighting such as WEKAF, Professor Joe Halbuna, Professor Max Pallen and GM Alfredo Bandalan. Angels Disciples helped to create rules for the original Northern Cal Escrima Association. All of the experience led me to create the United States Filipino Martial Arts Federation for Disney Martial Arts Festivals and with a start of a nonprofit organization and the help of my brother Gene Tibon and several volunteers this had become a reality at Anaheim Disney and Disney World Orlando Florida. The USFMAF lasted from 2006 to 2012. We also ran qualifiers in Stockton, Oregon and Arkansas with an opportunity to also run FMA divisions with the Long Beach Internationals. Throughout this time we had developed the most popular division of all, The Cultural Challenge. We offered this division at all of our tournaments. The late GM Narrie Babao who was a champion of this style in the late '70s and '80s was my guest of honor along with his wife, Zena and his son, Master Nar Babao. GM Narrie Babao was the man who inspired me to bring the Legacy Seminars to Southern California.

Guru Tibon, anything you'd like to mention?

I never dreamt that the Legacy series, honoring the GMs of FMA would grow to this many series. The FMA early pioneer escrimadors, we honor them and it is one of the greatest accomplishments in my life.

The Masters Hall of Fame induction in 2009, both me and my brother Gene Tibon Jr. were inducted at the same time for our respective arts and our life achievements of the martial arts, one of my most memorable achievements of my life. With this induction, I was also selected to be the Ambassador of FMA making my first selection of GM John Bais as well as receiving the induction. The following year, only to be the second time FMA was being introduced, was the biggest FMA selection to the Masters Hall of Fame.

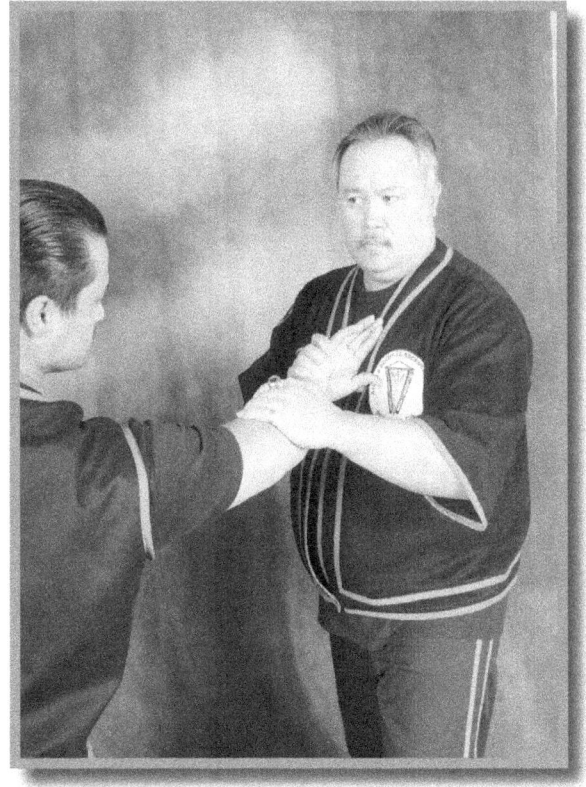

Four years later, 2014, I made another induction for the Masters Hall of Fame at the 50th Anniversary of the Long Beach International Tournament. In 2015 was my last selection as Ambassador for the Masters Hall of Fame.

I want to create opportunities to give to those who are deserving, help to promote and propagate those within the FMA world, create new barriers for the Filipino Martial Arts and throughout the FMA world. Lets make a positive opportunity for Filipino Martial Arts.

This is a very special thank you to all that have helped me succeed in this journey in my life of martial arts. Special thank you to my wife Darlene and my two kids, Desiree and my son Chez Tibon Sr., the longest standing student in the history of Angels Disciples and to Chezz Tibon Jr., my grandson, the youngest of Angels Disciples students, "Lil Z". The people that serve as my mentors a special thank you for helping me become the martial artist that I am today, thank you Dad, Gene Tibon Sr., my brother Gene Tibon Jr., Sonny Palabrica, Sensei Rodney Hu, and the late GM Angel Cabales. Special thank you to John Cabales for believing in me to have the strength to promote your dad's art Serrada Escrima and a special thank you for three decades of Angels Disciples students and affiliate chapters.

MARK V. WILEY

ON FILIPINO MARTIAL ARTS

MARTIAL ARTS GRANDMASTER, DOCTOR OF ORIENTAL MEDICINE, AUTHOR AND EDITOR, MARK V. WILEY IS IN A CLASS OF HIS OWN. HE BEGAN HIS MARTIAL ARTS TRAINING ALMOST 40 YEARS AGO AND HAS SINCE ACHIEVED MASTER-LEVEL IN THE FILIPINO ARTS OF CABALES SERRADA ESCRIMA, BINAS ARNIS, MODERN ARNIS, ESTALILLA KABAROAN ESKRIMA AND KALI ILLUSTRISIMO, AND IN THE CHINESE ARTS OF NGO CHO KUN AND WING CHUN KUEN.

SINCE 1994, DR. MARK HAS BEEN CONDUCTING EXTENSIVE TRAINING AND RESEARCH IN THE PHILIPPINES, MALAYSIA, SINGAPORE, TAIWAN AND JAPAN. DURING THAT TIME HE LIVED IN TOKYO AND MADE AN IMPRESSIVE 15 VISITS TO THE PHILIPPINES. IN 2000, HE WAS THE FIRST PERSON TO CONDUCT MARTIAL ART RESEARCH AMONG THE MATIGSALOG TRIBE OF MINDANAO, PHILIPPINES. DR. MARK HAS AUTHORED 12 BOOKS AND OVER 500 ARTICLES ON MARTIAL ARTS AND HOLISTIC HEALTH. HE SERVED AS EDITOR OF THE MAGAZINES MARTIAL ARTS ILLUSTRATED, MARTIAL ARTS LEGENDS, TAMBULI AND JOURNAL OF ASIAN MARTIAL ARTS, AND AS BOOK EDITOR AT CHARLES E. TUTTLE PUBLISHING COMPANY AND UNIQUE PUBLICATIONS. HE HAS ALSO HELD POSITIONS WITH ASIAN WORLD OF MARTIAL ARTS, I&I SPORTS AND WING LAM ENTERPRISES.

DR. MARK IS THE FOUNDER OF INTEGRATED ESKRIMA, PRESIDENT OF THE AMERICAN BENG HONG ATHLETIC ASSOCIATION, AND IS FORMER PRESIDENT OF THE FILIPINO WARRIOR ARTS ASSOCIATION. HE HAS BEEN NOMINATED TO SIX MARTIAL ARTS HALLS OF FAME IN THE CATEGORIES OF MASTER OF THE YEAR, WRITER OF THE YEAR AND WEAPONS INSTRUCTOR. HE IS NOT AFRAID TO MEET CONVENTION HEAD ON, WHICH HAS CREATED STIRS AND RIFFLED FEATHERS. POLITICS ASIDE, NO ONE CAN DIMINISH WHAT DR. MARK WILEY HAS GIVEN, AND CONTINUES TO GIVE, TO THE INTERNATIONAL MARTIAL ARTS COMMUNITY.

ESCRIMA MASTERS

How long have you been practicing the Filipino martial arts and who were/are your teacher?

I have been in the arts since 1979 and was fortunate to study directly under dozens of respected Filipino masters and grandmasters. The seven grandmasters who shared the most with me were Angel Cabales, Antonio Ilustrisimo, Herminio Binas, Remy Presas, Ramiro Estalilla, Benjamin Luna Lema, and Carlos Escorpizo.

How many styles (Eskrima or other methods) have you trained in?

Primarily I have trained extensively in the styles of the seven teachers mentioned above: Cabales Serrada Escrima, Kalis Ilustrisimo, Binas Dynamic Arnis, Modern Arnis, Estalilla Kabaroan Eskrima, Lightning Scientific Arnis, and Cinco Tero Arnis. Secondarily, there was also training in Balintawak, Kombatan, Moro-Moro Orabes Heneral, Arnis Lanada, Vee Arnis-Jitsu, JKD/Kali, Tabosa Kali Escrima, Pekiti Tirsia Kali, Lameco Eskrima, Doblete Rapellon (Mena) Arnis, Paete Arnis, Garimot Arnis, Siete Pares Arnis, Doce Pares Arnis, D'katipunan Arnis, Dekiti Tirsia Siradas, Lapunti Arnis de Abaniko, and many others to a lesser extent.

With regard to non-Filipino systems, I have spent 20 years in Ngo Cho Kun (Five Ancestor Fist) and 25 in Wing Chun Kuen, but also studied and earned black belts or teaching credentials in Tae Kwon Do, Boxe Francaise Savate, JKD Concepts, American Kenpo Karate. There are also styles in which I trained in Asia but did not pursue rank, such as: Indian Silambam and Marma Ati, Malay Silat Harimau and Seni Gayong, Chuka Phoenix-Eye Fist Kung-Fu, Tai Zu Quan, and White Crane. I am also currently involved at the basic levels of Okinawan Matayoshi Kobudo, learning under my good friend Russ Smith.

On a related note, I have embraced the Asian concepts and systems of medicine and healing and became a doctor of Traditional Chinese Medicine, Alternative Medicine, and practitioner of tui na, Thai yoga massage, herbal medicine, acupuncture, half a dozen systems of qigong (clinical and self-regulating), liangong, Vipassina meditation and other mind/body practices that balance the harm/heal paradigm along the path I follow.

Would you tell us some interesting stories of your early days in Escrima?

My earliest memory is of seeing a photo of the late GM Angel Cabales in Dan Inosanto's classic book, and reading the story Guru Dan shared about him. A small man with so much heart and fighting spirit.

I knew I had to train with him. When I began training with him, he was so gentle and kind, and would make me do everything in slow motion to get the timing and stick placement perfect. But when we demoed or sparred, it was fast and furious. Cabales would always say, "Anyone can play a song on the piano fast, but if they do it slow only a few can keep the proper time." I knew then, as a teenager, that he was expressing to me how vital timing is to the art. He also used to say, "Don't add things to my art or you will mix it up like spaghetti." The Serrada system is very tightly structured, and while you can create variations on its themes, to add movements that don't match the body type or movement style would "mix up" or confuse the efficiency of the techniques. I am not sure this holds for other FMA styles that are not so tightly structured in their movements; but it certainly holds true for Cabales Serrada Escrima.

I was also fortunate to study privately for ix years with Professor Herminio Binas, an old classic Arnis master from Negros Occidental, Philippines who retired in my home town of Philadelphia. He lived on South 17th Street in a tough neighborhood and I used to take the bus up to see him for training in him small row home. He was 79 years old and we started training espada y daga with wooden swords and daggers. As the years passed, this changed to light stair spindle railings. Then to plastic whiffle ball bat and short stick. He used to always lecture me on what he called "the humanitarian habitat." Be good to your neighbor, and he will be good to you. If you are attacked by an armed robber, just disarm him and do not harm him. Used locks and control and he will then become your friend. I used to wonder if this was the case. One day as I accompanied him down the street a few blocks to drop his granddaughter at the elementary school, we were approached by two guys. They gestured mean and demanded Master Binas' money. Out of nowhere he pulls this solid steel ball with a sting attached and swings it hard down on these guys' faces. The fell to the ground screaming and we kept walking. I was dumbfounded. Where did the weapon come from and what happened to "don't hurt your enemy"? LOL. When we got back to his home, Binas showed me his weapon and said he always keeps it in his pocket; it's less obvious than walking around with a stick. He also said, "When it's two or three on one, take them out!" LOL. I knew then, every rule was meant to be broken and each situation presented its own set of circumstances. Be prepared and don't try to be a hero when you can't.

Were you 'natural' at Eskrima – did the movements come easily to you?

I was not a natural, but I had an innate drive to master the art. I was already involved in other martial arts, but for whatever reason my focus and passion went into Eskrima. I created training devises in my home and would practice very hard. We lived in an apartment with those old coil heaters against the wall. I set a staff between the vertical coils and tied it in, and then tied a stick across it to make a cross pattern. I used to practice my counters on that when I didn't have a partner; which was most of the time then. Later I moved into a place that didn't have those coil heaters and used to jam sticks between the books on my shelves to practice on. Later I had people make different devices for me, like a spring loaded stick that would swing out from the wall hard and force me to block with a firm base stance. This was hard to do, and I would wear a motorcycle helmet or sparring helmet because sometimes I could not stop the blow with my block. Years later I was teaching sparring and was talking while a student swing at me and I blocked but my own stick reverberated back and smashed my eye and required stitches. Decades later the late Grandmaster Ben Lema was also injured in a similar situation, but during a challenge. I realized then the dangers of blocking over other defensive methods. Also that just because our training partners swing and stop their strike at the target and we can block and counter, an opponent will strike all the way through, and hard, trying to take your head off, and some of these block and counter methods just don't hold up. This all changed my impression and focus in my own training and path toward mastering Eskrima.

The modicum of skill I have developed is not a result of natural talent but of spending years hard training and studying the videos of the masters I trained with and interviewed, looking for similarities and differences in how they did each technique. I never wanted to be told I was good or hear things that supported what I was doing. You can't progress that way. I wanted to be hit and figure out why and how it was done to me. Which foot is forward? Does the stick move before the hips or not? What range is a certain technique best suited for? I felt like a scientist turning a microscope on these arts so that I could become skilled. So I think while many say I am a natural now at the age of 43, it was really a result of the detailed study I took to my learning and understanding of the arts from the time I was in my teens.

Today, because my expression of the art is based in controlling time and range to achieve a position of advantage – as opposed to being fast and honing my reflexes – I seem quick. But really my ability is from moving off the line of attack, controlling my range while pulling my opponent into an unfavorable range (even by a few inches), and not seeking to block the strikes coming at me but of moving myself into a safe gate while countering in the gaps between the opponent's techniques. You don't need to be a natural athlete to do this, only patient and in control of time and emotion.

How has your personal expression of Eskrima has developed over the years?

I have stopped learning other people's "styles" and I have stopped fussing over learning new techniques. I no longer think speed and highly developed reflexes are the way to master the art. But these are all things I used to focus on. I would say, Look how GM Cabales does his inside block (stick and live hand meet the weapon at the same time), versus GM Presas (stick and then hand in a sweeping motion) and would conclude that Cabales' was faster because there were fewer movements. I later realized this is only true to the extent of what is intended after the block, as no block is done in a vacuum but is part of a larger defensive technique or offensive/defensive/offensive action. So I began looking at each technique as a "study."

These days I also do not teach technique counters as the basis of applying Eskrima. I teach that strategy must lead everything. And part of that strategy is putting yourself is a favorable position relative to your opponent. While speed is good, it is not more important than timing. And while reflexes are necessary, they are not more important than being in a favorable position. After all, it's not how fast something travels but how soon it arrives! And it must arrive while you are not in a position to be countered; therefore alleviating the need for more reflexive responses. Controlling position and time form the basis of my application.

If you can control space (position and range) and you can control time, then you can move into gaps and counter without being countered (at least not as frequently). Many eskrimadores respond to an attack by positioning themselves to block the weapon and then counter. They lead their first move, reflexively, with a block or defense based on the angle of the attack coming at them. I do not. I notice the angle, but seek the space. Footwork is my defense, and the block or deflection is the secondary safety factor en route to striking my opponent. It is a very different approach, though looks the same to the outsider observing the action.

I have also categorized the techniques into what I called "Modes of Engagement." These are how quickly you can strike an opponent from the moment he attacks you. Mode 1 is direct striking, no block (on first movement); Mode 2 is simultaneous parry or pass with live hand while striking (hitting on first move but with left hand support); Mode 3 is intercepting the opponent's weapon with your weapon, redirecting it and countering all in one continuous movement (no left hand contact or block); and Mode 4 is all the two-to-three step block-then-counter techniques so common in the art (inside block, umbrella block, roof block). Even though most Eskrima styles teach and focus on Mode 4 techniques, they are actually the slowest and place you at disadvantage against a master of timing and positioning. I teach Mode 4 techniques last in my curriculum of basics.

Do you think different 'styles' are truly important in the art of Eskrima? Why?

Yes and no. Yes, because there needs to be a style, or more correctly a "system" in place to teach the art and one to train the art. But after one learns the techniques and develops skill he must not hold on to the style if it is detrimental to him becoming a better practitioner by self-expression.

No, because too many people get "suck" on the style and never truly grow as real artists within the arts. What's more, very few of these Eskrima styles continue on, like Chinese arts do, over generations. In China you can trace arts back hundreds and even thousands of years, but in the Philippines they can only be traced to 1920 or 1950 or 1980.

The research that I did up and down the Philippines showed me something very clear, and that is that there is only a few dozen techniques overall. There are less than a handful of disarming concepts, yet hundreds of "stylistic" variations on those concepts. There are only about 30 defensive techniques, yet hundreds of variations. So each "style" is basically a curriculum of a master who specialized in a few or more of the global techniques and created counters that the students memorize, and this becomes the style or expression of that master's Eskrima. If practitioners could understand and master the concept behind each movement (like the umbrella block or strip disarm, for example) then they could create hundreds of their own techniques. Many do this to an extent and think what they have done is to create a new style; but really they are just expressing the basic concept in their own way.

ESCRIMA MASTERS

What do you remember the most of all the masters you had the opportunity of training with?

GM Remy Presas was impressive to me for various reasons. He was very secure in his art, and didn't care the other Filipino masters in the US would ridicule him for "watering down" arnis for the general public. He brought the art out to the public in a huge way. Presas was actually quite fierce when sparring, and his techniques, though basic, were strong. Most impressively, he was equally skilled with both right and left hands. It was amazing to watch him switch hands and throw off his opponents in mid execution. Hi slocks were strong, too, and when he seized your wrist to disarm it was almost certain you could not counter before he took your weapon.

GM Angel Cabales was fearless. He had his principles and stood his ground against the rest of the West Coast Eskrima masters, and those who visited Stockton from other places and countries. He used a small stick, about 24-inches, but would say, "Even if your stick is a mile long, I can block it with 18 inches!" He knew he could bridge the gap and beat you, no matter what. And when he taught, it was all about precision in movement and timing to make that happen. There was intention in all of his moves and in every way he taught. His system is compact and has a progression to learning it, and includes entire studies of fainting techniques (picking), and counters to counters (reversals). He was also a masters of changing gates from inside to outside and vice versa to achieve position.

GM Antonio Ilustrisimo was the most impressive eskrimador I have seen. He was taller than most Filipinos and looked a bit lanky, but his skill was crafted in real encounters and with swords. He did not pay homage to the erroneous saying, "sticks and sword are the same." They are not, and when he engaged you with swords it was a much different story than when playing with sticks. He taught me to man-up and not be afraid to walk directly in toward the opponent's on-coming sword strike. Don't step back or zone away, but step right in and cut it off while hacking the opponent. This is so important I could write a book just on this concept and strategy. From this, it is easy to see why he feared no one and why his timing and positioning was so perfect. His art teaches direct striking, and little blocking. It teaches position and timing and how to wait out a strike until the last minute before countering, so the opponent doesn't "track" you and counter.

What was your first impression/feeling when began giving instruction in Japan?

I first visited Japan in 1994 and moved there the next year to serve as editor of the martial arts books at Charles E. Tuttle company. It was amazing to be in such a clean metropolis with such a history of martial arts. I visited sumo stadiums, museums, karate dojo, aikido hombu dojo, the Budokan, and lived walking distance from the Kodokan judo headquarters. I befriended a number of the late Donn Draeger's students, made new budo friends, watched demos at temples and observed classes everywhere I could.

I remember feeling humbled when asked to demonstrate Eskrima. But did so for Nishioka sensei of Jodo, and Nita sensei of Naginata, as well as for Diane Skoss, then editor of Aikido Journal and her husband Meik Skoss (Draeger student and sensei of Aikido and Naginata).

I loved teaching in Japan. My approach, and the Eskrima approach in general, is so much different than the Japanese approach. No katas, less structure, more informal, more free flow to counters. Some of this is good and some not so good, but different nonetheless.

How different from other Martial Arts styles do you see the principles and concepts of Eskrima?

The main difference is that Eskrima is an application art. This gives its practitioners a distinct advantage to being able to use the arts right away, even against unpredictable attacks. Reflexes and responses to all numbers of attacks, with weapons and without weapons, disarms, locks and more are all taught right away. Aside from some of the modern styles of Eskrima, that borrowed their teaching method from Japanese and Korean systems, there is little solo practice or line-drills or repetitions of moves in Eskrima. It is mainly taught in application against attacks from day one.

Many, if not most, other arts teach basics, strikes, stances, one-steps in the beginning. It takes a long time to break the mold and begin to move reflexively and spontaneously against uncooperative opponents or partners. In many styles, the sparring (which is sport or recreational based) does not coincide with the basic blocks and kata movements or even the one-step defenses taught in the same class. There is disconnect between the means of training and the hoped-for usability of the art in the end result.

There are good and bad points to both approaches. Overall, I see a lack of basics and fundamental skill among some eskrimadores, especially the seminar taught ones in the West. They have plenty of application skill but less in the realms of body structure, balance, rooting, detailed minutia of technique. On the other hand, many other systems have very strong foundations, but are unable to apply them in realistic settings. And sparring techniques are not the same as the fighting or defensive techniques they teach in their forms or line drills. If the two approaches could meet up, I believe both Filipino and non-Filipino styles would benefit.

Do you think that Eskrima in the West has 'caught up' with the technical level in the Philippines?

It has become noticeably different, actually. Eskrima in the Philippines is still, for the most part, "pure." What I mean by this is, while the art is growing and expanding there, the techniques still look like Eskrima, and follow the principles of Eskrima, and the blocks and counters retain their flavor and basis.

In the West, the art is almost always mixed with JKD or Kenpo or Silat or Wing Chun. As a result, it does not look like "pure" Eskrima, even though the practitioners are doing the same movements. The balance is difference, the center of gravity is moved from the waist up to the chest, the strikes are not as clean, and the execution is blurred with non-specificity. It is easy for me to identify who has trained in an Eskrima system from the beginning and who learned in seminars and mixed it because the flavor is not the same.

ESCRIMA MASTERS

Skill wise, both are good. When the art is infused with large quantities of techniques from other systems here in the West, there is advantage. But without the "through line" or "spine" on which to implement or connect those within Eskrima proper, there becomes a lack of ability to execute in a way that is truly solid. Again, the ability to blow through lock flows and 20 move counters, takedowns is not really an example of highly developed skill. Thus, I would say the technical skill among practitioners in the Philippines is better than here in the US (notwithstanding those who trained in a pure Filipino art under a properly trained master). But the overall quantity of techniques taught within Eskrima in the West is greater.

Eskrima and Arnis are nowadays often referred to as a sport... would you agree with this definition?

Yes, for the most part because it is taught and practiced as a past-time, a hobby, and with sport rules to score points in the tournaments. Not everyone trains that way, but it is becoming more and more popular. What is important is not to confuse sport skill with fighting or self-defense skill. They are different and require a different set of attributes and training methods. Therefore, how one is teaching the art should be made known to the students so if they are learning sport Eskrima, they don't think it is fighting Eskrima. It's all about managing expectations and keeping true to what you get out of the art based on your personal goals and interests.

Do you feel that you still have further to go in your studies of the art?

Of course. But I don't think anyone or any style has a new technique I have not seen. Everything is a variation on a theme and once the concepts are learned the rest are examples of them. However, I have struggled to teach my art in a way that is easy for people to "get" and digest. I teach beginners and also grandmasters of different arts, and even within Eskrima, and it takes them a while to understand what I am sharing. I think because my approach is rooted in theory and strategy and principles and not in techniques, the thought process is hard to follow. They can repeat the technique I show them as an "example" of the theory, but are at a loss to create a technique on their own that also follows the theory. So I am now, and have been for a while, on a quest to learn and improve my methods of imparting the "marrow" of the art and have been taking guidance from several mentors in how to make it more easily learned. I don't see what is so difficult, but my formal students and seminar students and other masters can see what I am doing but have trouble doing it themselves. And the responsibility for making it "learnable" is on me. So I have still a ways to go there.

How different do you see the training attitude in the U.S. when compared to the Philippines?

I see a huge difference in attitude, and it is cultural. Overall in the West, there is a lack of respect shown to peers, parents, teachers, elders and many feel entitled to get what they want and to get it now. In the East, though the trend is changing a bit, the tenet of respect plays a huge factor in daily life. In the Philippines, even when they call their teacher by his first name, they include "master" or "sir" or another word with it. In the West, it's first name we are the same, too loose. As a result, in the West many practitioners (and this was true for me for a time), want to be masters and heads of their own arts right away. They also think they've created a new system because they changed some things or added new techniques, not realizing these are just examples of the concept in the original art anyway. They want to be on top and they want it now and the less they need to train the better. This is not true for everyone, of course, but it is a trend over here. In the Philippines, the attitude is mostly one of humility, respect for the art and the teacher, and self restraint. I like that.

Do you have any general advice you would care to pass on the practitioners in general?

Your time and efforts are better spent studying the basics and making a study of each technique. Learn how to apply the techniques in the right range, and gate, and mode, and time. Don't rush, there is plenty of time. Avoid the trap of accumulating vast numbers of techniques and thinking that you are an expert because of the "width" of your repertoire. Depth is more important. Each technique must be learned and developed with "depth," or the things that anchor it and make it usable, like body structure, foot placement, distance, timing, weapon juxtaposition. Don't just "swing wood" but instead make a

ESCRIMA MASTERS

point of doing everything on purpose and for a reason. If your right foot is forward and your wrist is turned a certain way when striking, do that on purpose and know the reason for it. Mastery of any art is found in perfecting the details.

Some people think going to the Philippines to really progress in the art is highly necessary, do you share this point of view?

Yes, but not as necessary if you have had the opportunity to train with a Filipino master who was born and raised in the Philippines and are able to study his system from the bottom up, over time. The art is still taught that way in the Philippines, but not so much in the US, where most of those elder masters who brought this method here have passed away. Some exceptions would be those masters (of whatever nationality) who did study the art under a master who brought it over here, like those in Stockton or Los Angeles or Hawaii or New York or Philadelphia. Getting into a school or club that follows the old teaching is the key.

However, to be able to put the art in cultural perspective and to see many more styles and masters than are known here in the West, going to the Philippines is invaluable. It was for me all 13 times I've been there. The pitfall, that I have seen again and again, is practitioners from the West going to the Philippines, and only attending a tournament and training with their teacher there. Also, going with a "full cup" and thinking you know it all and viewing other arts with the lens of how you can beat them or that you already know their art, is a net loss. Be humble, be open minded, seek out other systems and experiences, and don't do in the Philippines what you can do already in the West and the trip can be of huge value.

What are the aspects you think Westerners practitioners advantage their Philippines counterpart?

They want to advance the art and expand it and have so many other arts at their disposal to vet it against. Also, the techniques in sports training in general play a big part. Here it is ok to train in many arts with many teachers, as most learn Eskrima in seminars anyway. This is a drawback as mentioned, but also offers advantages in terms of exposure and vetting of skill. I hope a better middle ground can be achieved.

What would you say to someone who is interested in starting to learn Eskrima?

First know what your goals are and find a school or teacher who can help you achieve them. If you want realistic training for fighting or law enforcement, then a sport style will not serve this end. And if you have no interest in killing techniques or hard core training, then a more casual style for hobby or sports is better suited.

What do you see as the most important attributes of a student?

Patience, self-discipline, restraint and respect.

What are your thoughts on the future of the art?

I would love to see a renaissance of the classic styles. I would love for those who have added to the art techniques from other systems, and those who learned from seminars primarily, to have the opportunity to study anew a classical system from the ground up. With this, I think in the West, Eskrima can develop and advance in a better way, structurally. In the Philippines, there is a history since the late 1940s of advancing the art with other methods (like karate, judo and aikido). If the Philippines can drop the colonial mentality and trust in their own national treasure, then they

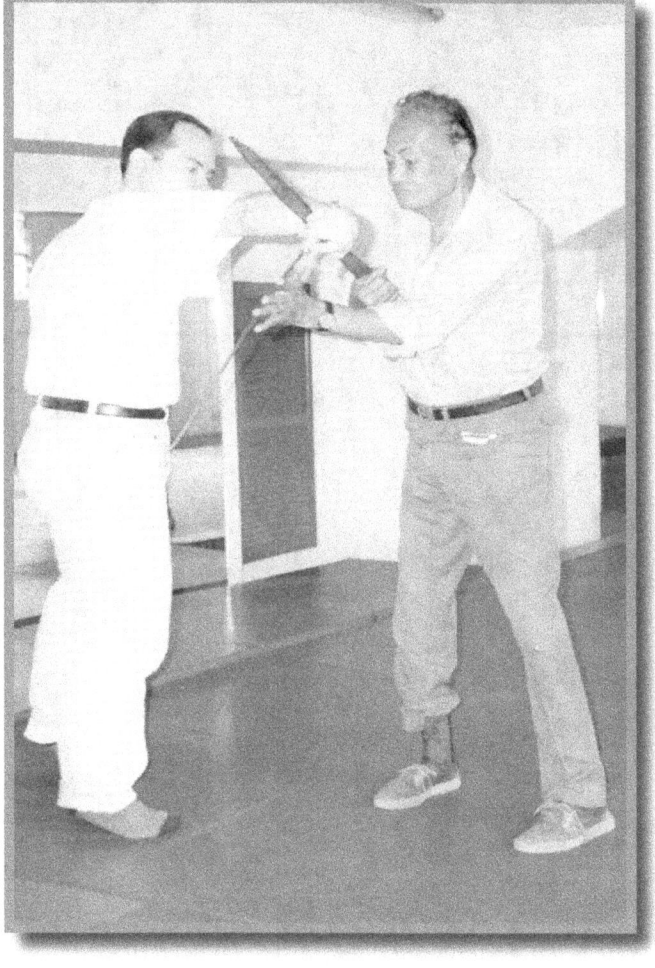

can advance the arts vetting against more styles without adding those styles to Eskrima. In other words, adjusting the training and developing out principles to accommodate the techniques from other arts, without thinking the others are better and dropping their basics for them.

Eskrima is a treasure and can be a valuable life study. With a proper understanding and patience and a desire to learn, you can come to know yourself through the art and know the art through yourself. And so the future of the art can parallel the future of each practitioner individually.

EPILOGUE

ESCRIMA

THE HIDDEN TREASURE

BY ANTONIO E. SOMERA

IT HAS BEEN MORE THAN 35 YEARS SINCE DAN INOSANTO INTRODUCED THE WORLD TO THE FILIPINO MARTIAL ARTS, AND IT TOOK GURO DAN NEARLY 15 YEARS BEFORE THAT TO LEARN THE MARTIAL ARTS OF HIS ANCESTORS. ENCOURAGEMENT FROM HIS LATE TEACHER AND GOOD FRIEND SIFU BRUCE LEE TOO SEEK OUT HIS ROOTS OF MARTIAL ARTS AND TO LEARN OF THE MANY UNSUNG MASTER IN THE ARTS WAS THE MISSION OF YOUNG INOSANTO. WITHOUT A DOUBT, HIS GROUNDBREAKING BOOK, THE FILIPINO MARTIAL ARTS AS TAUGHT BY DAN INOSANTO, WOULD OPEN THE DOOR AND WOULD BE THE REFERENCE BOOK AND INSPIRATIONAL GUIDE FOR MANY STUDENTS AND TEACHERS TO SEEK OUT THE MASTERS AND THE MANY DIFFERENT STYLES OF FILIPINO MARTIAL ARTS THAT INOSANTO FEATURED IN THIS NOW HARD TO FIND COLLECTOR'S BOOK. THIS POWERFUL BOOK WAS A WEALTH OF INFORMATION THAT EXPOSED THOUSANDS OF READERS TO AN ART THAT WAS LOST FROM FILIPINO SOCIETY HERE IN AMERICA. THIS BOOK TRULY WOULD INSPIRE COUNTLESS READERS TO RESEARCH FURTHER AND TO SEEK ADDITIONAL INFORMATION ON THE FILIPINO MARTIAL ARTS.

The names of humble men that the world has never heard of before would become Filipino Martial Arts icons, a kind of Superstars to America and eventually to the world. These men also would become role models, father figures, and men who would change the life destinies of thousands upon thousands of people and would find a new found respect for the Filipino community and its hidden Martial Arts.

The Filipino Martial Art treasures Inosanto uncovered for America and the world would be men by the names of Pepe Montano Arca and Vincent Arca, escrima instructors who came to the Hawaiian Islands and eventually would accompany the first Filipino immigrants who, without knowing it, would kept the art alive:

Pepe Montno Arca was Inosanto's grandfather; Master Pedro Apilado was known as one of the top fighters and would serve as head referee in the Hawaiian Islands in the days when full contact stick fighting was done without armor; Master Apilado also was a student under the great champion of the Northern Philippines, Santiago Toledo; the famous Canete family would have the largest escrima school

in the Philippines; Grand Master Angel Cabales, considered the man responsible for the exposure of escrima to the American public, was most effective with the short stick and was a true master of the art; Master Regino Ellustrisimo a master in the Bohol method of escrima; Grand Master Leo M. Giron, a man with a wealth and knowledge of the combative art of arnis escrima whose combat proven style was tested during World War II for more than a year in the jungles of the Philippines (Insoanto would consider Leo Giron to be his second father).

Also, Grand Master Juanito Lacoste, considered by Inosanto to be the most well-rounded escrimador and a master of stick, dagger, long blade, and empty hands; Grand Master Ben Largusa, the most all-around Filipino Kali martial artist, according to Inosanto, and a student of the great Grand Master Floro Villabrille, champion of countless matches in the Philippines and Hawaii; Master Pasqual Ovales, the grandson of the great Santiago Toledo, a master in the Toledo-Collando style of escrima that uses the long stick and "escala" (stroking pattern) of training; Grand Master Braulio Pedoy, who taught escrima but also the awareness of the history of the Filipino martial art and culture; Master Narrie Babao, who holds the title of champion in the first weapons sparring tournament held in the United States; Grand Master Lucky Lucay Lucay, whose expertise is in "Sikara (Filipino Foot Fighting) and Panatukan (Filipino Boxing).

Also on the list are Master Dentoy Revillar, senior student of Grand Master Cabales and the first to train with both Cabales and Giron, making him highly efficient in both the short and long stick methods, and an organizer in the first escrima academy open to the public in the United States; Grand Master Jack Santos, who serves as an advisor to the Filipino Kali Academy in Torrance; Master Max Sarmiento, a man gifted with the use of empty hands, dagger, and knives, who was one of the first, along with his wife Lynn, to help organize the Cabales academy, the first open to the general public in the United States; Grand Master Telesporo Subing Subing, an expert in the Moro style and double stick style of the Southern Philippines; Grand Master Sam Tendencia, who trained under the great Deogracias Tipace in the Philippines and is expert in the art of Filipino

nerve pinching and Hilot (massage); Grand Master Gilbert Tenio, who trained in many Filipino arts and was founder of the Tenio Dequedas system in Stockton, California; Grand Master Floro Villabrille of Hawaii, known as the undefeated champion in countless escrima and kali matches in the Philippines and Hawaii; And Grand Master Viliabrille, who at that time was the head of the Kali organization.

Add to the group Grand Master Richard Bustillo, who during that time was Inosanto's training partner and also was responsible for promoting and preserving the Filipino Martial Arts and Jeet Kune Do; Ed Parker, Inosanto's instructor in Kenpo karate and in Inosanto's opinion a "true Master," And last but not least the great Sifu Bruce Lee, who was Inosanto's instructor and good friend who guided him to the art of Jeet Kune Do. Under Sifu Lee's tutelage, Inosanto gained the educational eye to find out what was functional in the Martial Arts. Lee also encouraged Inosanto to look for his roots in the arts and to continue until he has found all that is useful.

Guro Dan Inosanto's book The Filipino Martial Arts was so powerful that many individuals followed in his footsteps in researching the Filipino Martial Arts. It is a virtual encyclopedia of unadventured knowledge exposed to the public for our own consumption. Thousands more would experience the art itself and would test the very foundation of the applications of techniques.

After all the research and information publish on the Filipino Martial Arts, you would think that we would have exhausted our wealth of individuals who would play the art of our forefathers. Digging a little deeper in my hometown that once was called "Little Manila" because of the huge Filipino population, Stockton, California, would be the small farming community that to this date still would have a few more hidden treasures.

These men now are the last of their kind, the ancient ones who set the foundation for us to have a better life here in America. These men are still active; some teaching the Filipino Martial Arts and others would be more than happy to demonstrate and tell stories about the many different styles of the Filipino arts.

Jesus Ragail Corales was born in Narvacan, Illocos Sur Philippines on December 25, 1910. Like Giron, Corales arrived in America in 1929. He immediately took a bus from San Francisco to Stockton and would work in the fields and farm labor camps in the San Joaquin valley. Due to his working in the many different Filipino labor camps, he would be exposed to a number of Filipino escrimadors. Corales would take the time to play or train in the art after a hard day's work in the fields. He remembers that "after working so hard during the day, in the afternoon, during a cool delta breeze, my town mates and I would sit outside next to the barn away from everyone and play with our asparagus or sticks knives. I can remember the quickness of the weapon but no one would get hurt." Corales' teacher was a man by the name of Hilario Ramolete from Santa Catalina Illocos Sur, Philippines. Corales played the cabaroan or new system of arnis escrima. His specialty was the cinco tero style or five strikes; also the redonda style or circular striking, and close quarter hand-to-hand combat. Corales was a member of the 1st Filipino Regiment and served in the invasion of Lyette, Philippines, during World War II. Of the four in this article, Corales had the most energy. At times, it was difficult to interview him and also play with him because he would keep moving. He would explain

his current movement and would already be demonstrating the next movement. His knowledge of the Filipino arts of self-defense is unlimited as his energy to demonstrate it. Corales is also a member of one of the "Big Three" Filipino Lodges of America, The Caballeros de Dimas Alang.

Joe Arruejo Pacpaco was born in Vigan Illocos Sur Philippines on November 24, 1909. He arrived in San Francisco in 1930 on the President Jefferson and went to Stockton by boat through the San Joaquin Delta. As did most of the Filipinos who arrived during this first wave, Pacpaco took his first job cutting celery. He also worked in the many different Filipino farm labor camps in the San Joaquin Valley and occasionally took work in Marysville and Yuba City, California. Pacpaco's teacher was a man by the name of Francisco Realin from Santa Catalina, Philippines. His system of play is the cabaroan or new style of arnis escrima. His style is Larga Mano or long hand/weapon style; he also plays abierta or open body style of arins escrima and he has an empty hand style that is similar to cadena de mano. Pacpaco's Larga mano is different from Leo Giron's larga mano. Pacpaco incorporates the abierta (open) body footwork to his larga mano. Pacpaco's footwork is attributed to his natural open foot movement. Joe Pacpaco has a unique gift of playing. He is left-handed, very graceful and to the point. Pacpaco and Giron would play together in the Giron's basement and at the Filipino Grand Lodge just half a block from both Pacpaco and Giron's house and a block from Inosanto's house. Pacpaco was the person that Giron had in mind to train the "killer" style to Dan Inosanto. Pacpaco is also a life member of the Legionarios Del Trabajo and member of the Worshipful Mabini Lodge with over 60 years of service to the Filipino lodge.

Victorino Ton was born June 29, 1895, in Lapaz Abra, Philippines. He arrived in Hawaii in 1924 and worked in the pineapple and sugar cane plantations for six years. After completing his work contract in Hawaii he moved on to Stockton, California in 1930. Ton's first job in Stockton was cutting asparagus. To my knowledge, Victorino Ton is the oldest living arnis escrima player in America. At the time of this article Ton was 108 years old and lived at a Filipino lodge in Stockton, enjoying a very simple life, gardening, and playing cards. The first question he had for me was, "why are we so close?" and the second question was, "do I have a longer weapon"? This would lead me to believe he was a cabaroan (new style) escrimador. Ton plays the cinco tero (five strikes) and incorporates blocking and counter striking. He started playing with sticks in the Philippines at the age of 10; this would be 1905. This was without a doubt one of the most fertile times of escrimadors in Philippine history due to the Filipino revolution. Ton is truly a son of the revolution who fought against the Spaniards in the Filipinos' struggle to gain their freedom from Spain. Manong Ton also is a life member of the Legionarios del Trabajo in America and is a member of General Lim lodge with more than 60 years of service to the Filipino lodge.

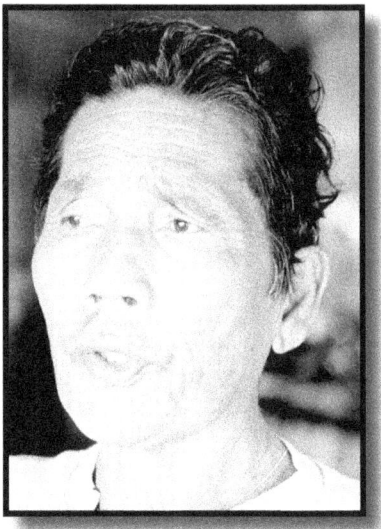

I would like to mention a few factors that link these four incredible men together.

1. They all came to America during the first wave of Filipinos from the Philippines.
2. They all were farm laborers.
3. They all learned and still practice the Filipino Martial Arts.
4. They all are members of a Filipino Masonic Lodge.
5. They are all from Luzon, Philippines.

Amazingly enough, these hidden treasures are still with us today.

Many thanks to our forefathers like Giron, Corales, Pacpaco, and Ton who endured so many hardships to make our life better. And for those Grand Masters and Masters of the arts, Cabalas, Elustrisimo, Giron, LaCoste, Largusa, Villarille, Canete, Tenio, Pedoy, Tabosa, Ovales, Santos, Revillar, Sarmiento, Lucaylucay, Babao, Paker, Subing Subing, Tendencia, (others that I have not mentioned please forgive me) and the legendary Bruce Lee.

And thanks to people like Inosanto, Bustillo, Lucaylucay, and Dentoy Revillar for helping our generation recognize our Filipino fathers and our heritage. The torch has been passed to us to continue with their work and to ensure the legacy of our forefathers will live on forever.

www.ingramcontent.com/pod-product-compliance
Lightning Source LLC
Chambersburg PA
CBHW081723100526
44591CB00016B/2481